CANYON
Breezes

CANYON
Breezes

Exploring Magical Places in Nature

JOSEPH COLWELL

Lichen Rock Press
Hotchkiss, Colorado 81419

Design: Constance King Design
Cover photography: Katherine Colwell

Lichen Rock Press
Hotchkiss, Colorado
ColwellCedars.com

ISBN: 978-0-9962222-0-4
Printed in USA

AUTHOR'S INVITATION

Though we travel the world over to find the beautiful,
we must carry it within us or we find it not.

~ Ralph Waldo Emerson ~

I invite you on an adventure of discovery and insight into nature drawn from over 45 years of observation while working and exploring throughout the West, penning thoughts about what I have seen and what inspires me.

Influenced by John Muir, Sigurd Olson, Aldo Leopold, Loren Eiseley, and many others, I look beyond the obvious to ask questions about what makes our world and its history so mysterious and magical. Curious to a fault, I cannot be satisfied with simple answers. What makes the natural world? What makes living things behave as they do? What makes humans behave as we do?

I have explored California's North Coast, the trails of Mount Rainier, the slickrock canyons of Southern Utah, the high peaks of the Colorado Rockies, and the forests of South Dakota's Black Hills—always asking questions, be it to the chickadees at feeders or the cougar that haunt the wilds.

I find magical moments in nature. The wild areas contain hidden secrets; so too, the city parks and our very own backyards. Join me in these stories of personal exploration, and may you be inspired to find your own special places.

Joseph Colwell, March 30, 2015
Hotchkiss, Colorado

CONTENTS

CANYONS

*This is the most beautiful place on earth.
There are many such places. Every man, every
woman, carries in heart and mind the image of the
ideal place, the right place, the one true home,
known or unknown, actual or visionary.*

~ Edward Abbey, *Desert Solitaire* ~

ON THE RIM

As I sat on the rim looking out over the expanse of rock and canyons, I tried to compose some colorful description. But the result was similar to what I was looking at. A universe of nothing. Space and time. The wonder of the Moab canyon country is beyond words. This was one of those things that could not be described. Sure, I could compose adjectives and metaphors that were filled with the ethereal, the poetic. But in the end, it would be only hyperbole. I could try and describe my philosophical musings. That didn't even work. I tried anyway.

My wife and I found a secluded edge of the plateau south of Moab and drove an easy four wheel track through the slickrock and juniper. Parking at the end of the marked county road, just feet away from the rim, we put the dog on a leash and picked our way along the sandstone, avoiding the cryptobiotic soil. Forget the view just off to our left, I thought, as we played hide and seek with the scene through the trees. Walking along the remnants of a four wheel drive track that continued on from where we parked was easy satisfaction. The slickrock was broken occasionally by the sand that passed for soil. Vegetation on this warm spring day was in full bloom. The desert can indeed bloom and its diversity was uplifting. Pinhook cactus was in purple splendor, cliff rose was in seductive flower. Red was overwhelming in the soil and its parent rock. Swirls and undulations marked the sandstone; crusty cryptobiotic blankets of soil indicated a protective microscopic universe at my feet.

But the edge of the rim always beckoned. The world fell away into that abyss of sky. The view was magnetic. The entire world once looked like this. It was the view God had when she contemplated what to do next. The ravens mocked me and my kind as they played aerial tag above the edge of forever. I was earthbound, although the temptation was there in the background to join them in one glorious leap. I tucked that thought aside, holding onto the rock. I wanted to be part of the cliff, part of the solid yet tenuous thing called earth.

Wise people say the color green is soothing. The green of the cactus and juniper, single leaf ash and Indian ricegrass was indeed soothing. But the reds and oranges and maroons and tans that painted the view below me were not so much soothing as primal. They were the earth itself, the very essence of everything there is. This was the universe, pulled together from space dust. Star stuff in its poetic form. It was time and space woven into a magic that neither I nor anyone who has ever walked this planet has ever been able to fathom.

My mind flew over the expanse of canyons and plateaus. I wanted to fully understand this display, but as has always happened in southern Utah, I couldn't. The element of time, the millions of years that I saw on display, overpowered my senses. Something in the far dark recesses of history started it all. Then that something melted and disappeared, reassembling itself into the rocks that buried each other in a span of time that I cannot understand.

Then another expanse of time passed while rain and wind unpeeled all that work. Now I was looking out over the missing rocks and dunes and mudflats and seafloors of this same world that no human has ever been part of.

What I was mesmerized by was not what was there. It was what wasn't there. Space sitting amongst eons of time. I suppose I could look out into outer space and think the same thing. Suns and planets and galaxies may have been there once and now had all disappeared and reassembled into these rocks and me. That is a degree of space that someday I may contemplate from a viewpoint such as I had here, but it is so far beyond my ability to understand, we will leave that for another day and another lifetime.

I measure time by minutes and days and years, but it is not unlimited. I will see less than one hundred winters. This view encompasses hundreds of millions of tropical, snowless winters. How can I or anyone ever grab hold of that? The fact that it is all beyond any of us, even the Einsteins and Sagans of the world, is what compels me to it. For a member of a species that prides itself in finding answers, even the ability to ask the questions, it is the ultimate test of knowledge that I admit there are no answers. There are not even intelligent questions. How can there be? You cannot look at this view and not believe in that all powerful force, call it God or simply the wind and time. It is a power that creates stars and universes, yet has time and imagination to sculpt rocks and rivers and junipers and cactus flowers into infinite detail. How can the two be the product of the same hand? It includes both the expanse of infinity and the delicate purple flower petals surrounded by thorny spines, toughing it out in this hostile expanse of sand and dry heat. Life and non-life. Yet they are all the same. How do you separate one from another?

I tried to fit adjectives and metaphors into sentences. I failed like everyone else who has tried. There was no use to take a photograph, paint a picture, write a poem. There was also no use to think grand philosophic thoughts, although that was where I ended. In the meantime, I gawked in awe, amazed, humbled, puzzled. No radio or music, not even conversation interrupted my thoughts. I was aware of only the wind and the cry of a raven, the rustle of a lizard, the sound of the sunlight bouncing off the cliff. I realized I was in conversation with my maker, one on one. At times serious, at times humorous. It is all the same. Time and space. It changes one; you cannot come back from the edge and be the same. You only go on, thinking that someday, somewhere, in another life or universe, maybe you can understand it all. But for that May morning, I just stared into the missing world, the time gone by, and breathed that same oxygen that rusted the iron of a lost age and created red rock. Oxygen which created and destroyed and reassembled rock and mud, trees and dinosaurs, mountains and seafloors.

I returned from my flight into time, out of space. I looked around, tearing free from the hypnotic view. I saw again the rock I was sitting on. Sensuously smooth, red orange with swirls and streaks, polished by wind and rain and the caresses of sunlight filling the blue vastness of sky. The ground gently sloped upward, away from the edge of itself, stair stepped by rock and sandy soil, junipers and cactus. Walk a few hundred yards and the soil deepened, the rock sank into the hidden expanse that belied anything unusual below the sandy surface. On the plateau, grass and sage thickened into an undulating ocean of life that was satisfied to await its time. At some point in the distant future, the canyon rim would crawl back, exposing a rock clad rim that would replace the one I sat on. My comfortable seat would be hanging in the open space I was so awed by. The abyss would be larger, the void deeper, the world evolving grain of sand by grain of sand.

The wind would continue to rustle the juniper branches, the lizards would scamper by pleasantly ignorant of the changing world around them. It would be the same world I was familiar with, but by then I would be floating the universe seeking new answers. Atoms of oxygen and phosphorous that were once me, freed from the gravity of this planet, would seek the company of a companion now millions of miles away. A new star would grab onto the quarks that once wondered about time and space. A new earth would coalesce and after time, another being would ponder the meaning of what it saw. And there would probably still be no correct answers to the questions created by space and time.

I eased back into the truck, started the engine, and we drove away. The ravens still soared above the edge of their known universe. I smiled at them with envy.

ARCHES

I went to church today. It had been years since I stood beneath the towers, the walls, and the sacredness of this red and orange temple. I used to live not many miles from here, breathing and sleeping within the churchyard expanse.

My church is as sacred as any cathedral, even John Muir's holy temple of Hetch Hetchy and the high Sierra. It is the sacred rock of Edward Abbey, if he held anything sacred.

I returned to the red rock temples of Arches National Park. It was hard, even on this late October Friday, to find any silence, any space to myself. I didn't have the time to wander off where that quiet still exists. I had to make do with a two hour vesper service, only a promise. A promise as elusive as the call of the canyon wren. But it had to suffice. Promises do that.

I thought of Abbey, who sat here decades ago, composing his thoughts, creating his prayers, devising his irreverence. He thought this part of Utah to be the most beautiful place on Earth. I heard his very soul bouncing off the Entrada cliffs like an echo reverberating with the freedom and openness which he said encouraged real love. He was now able to do that, ignoring the crowds of unseeing tourists treading through his land. He could avoid those visitors unable to hear his own laughter or the scolding of the ravens and their own shadows bouncing off the glowing sunset red of the sandstone.

He is one with his creator now, oblivious to the desecration he would see in all our natural cathedrals. I turned my thoughts to that creator. How can you not, as you stand here in awe of the majesty of red rock, believe in God and bow to her mighty works? If you choose not to believe in a god, then you marvel even more at the magnificence of nature in this place. Either way, you stand humbled by the rock, the red stone thrusting into the electric blue of the October sky.

I watched the latest group of hikers, cameras in hand, laughing as they walked. Did they see the sculpted cliffs, varnished black by fingers of stain creeping down the wall? Did they hear the scolding of the chickadee, flittering from juniper to serviceberry? If not, I brand them the most banal of atheists. I could no more spit on the floor of the Sistine Chapel, not holy to my own personal faith, than I could walk under these cliffs without thanking my creator.

And the creation itself! My, what talent in forming these rocks sand grain by sand grain. Can you see the patterns, the swirls, the color, the texture? And those grains, reused from earlier rock, cemented by tender touches to a solid sea of sand. Then, in a fit of patient idleness, time not in millennia but in ageless eons, my creator eroded her sculpture grain by grain back to the very red field of drifted sand now lying across this landscape. My creator made a three dimensional work of art, then made another work of even more profound sculpture as she tore it apart. Abbey might have seen the perfection, but he also derided our ignorance of it. I was able to ignore this insolence by most visitors; I managed to hold back the tears of shame. The tears which came of joy, of wonder, of humility washed the other sorrow away.

As I sat under one of the nameless cliffs, I listened to the chatter of the chickadee. This was not a wonder to him. It was his home. He knew no other. His entire life,

every waking moment, was spent flying under these red
cathedral walls. And to him, they were indeed nameless
cliffs, trees, and rock formations. I was dizzied and lost
in the names when I realized I was actually lost in the
importance of names. Wingate or Entrada? It was red
sandstone; that is all that matters. Formed by boundless
Sahara dunes, or ripple sculpted river bottom. You look
at the cliff and think "Entrada," and you walk away
satisfied. Take away the name and you look at the rock
walls and see the swirls of grains, the rounded cliffs of
sensuous bumps and curves, the stains of old rock and
fresh scabs where new angular boulders lay at the base,
ready to soften their edges with each new raindrop. What
is in a name?

The chickadee fluttered over a serviceberry into a dead
juniper. He didn't know the names. Calling it a serviceberry
hid your ability to see the October gold of the round leaf
in the process of twirling to the ground, covering the earth
with a golden speckled blanket. It was a bush like many
others, yet itself a sculpture of twigs, twisted and curved
upward and outward. Leaves dotted it like a Van Gogh
painting. I wanted to toss out my curiosity, framed by years
of scientific naming, to cry out: "I don't care who you are!
You are green and gold and red." Swirls and angles and
dots of sound and color in this hallowed place. We are blind
enough to all this; let's not narrow the blinders even more.

The chickadee, ignoring me with a mix of disdain and
apathy, flew off across the red sand, below the red cliff,
into the yellow bush. I smiled. Time was up. I had to leave.
I listened for Abbey to bounce his curses off another cliff,
into the open arch, out into the blinding sun on the other
side. I was the intruder to the yellow bush, to the small
black and white whirlwind of a bird, and to the red walls
of stone. I will come again, nameless to these walls. Then,

I will find a quiet spot, miles from another of my own species. I will be just another observer, like the October breeze. Maybe then I will learn the real names.

LOST IN THE ROCKS OF TIME

I can see Boulder Mountain, that behemoth of southern Utah, looming on the horizon just a few miles from where I sit, partway up Thousand Lake Mountain, its neighbor to the north. It seems like I have climbed halfway to heaven from the Fremont Valley just outside of Bicknell, but a knob called the Anthill on the side of the mountain is still an unreachable goal above me.

This is one of my favorite journeys. I drive from my house in Bicknell a mile towards Sunglow Campground, park the car, then climb and scramble up the Wingate cliff. Once on top of the cliff, I stop to rest, let my heart slow its pounding, then wander across the level pinyon juniper grassland, deftly avoiding the cryptogamic soil. This biological wonder of the Colorado Plateau is part of the living breathing soil. Technically a combination of algae, fungi, moss, and who knows what else, this crust is a delicate, sensitive cover of the never ending red soil. I must show respect since a simple footprint can destroy it. Walking through this protective soil cover can be time consuming. I need to slow down.

The crust is long-lived, possibly as old as the ancient forests of bristlecone pine five hundred miles west of here. Look at it closely. There are hoodoos and spires, valleys and caverns on a miniature scale. It lives and breathes, grows and creeps across the sand, absorbing the thundering raindrops of the July storm and soaking up the melting snow of the February blizzard. It gently shelters the sand from the howling March winds and snuggles up to the alligator skin bark of the gnarled juniper, itself snuggling up to the red sandstone. I think back to the rhyme I chanted in my childhood as I skipped down the sidewalk, "step on a crack, break your grandmother's back." Modify that to "step on those cryptogam things, break an angel's wings." I have to move on. I will never get anywhere if I stop to contemplate everything I see.

This plateau, as far as I can tell, has no easy access. It is red sand, juniper, cactus, and Indian ricegrass, but it is wilderness for me, as surely as if it were in the middle of Alaska. I see no sign of civilization; I hear only the pinyon jays and ravens, and I'm only an hour away from the comfort of home.

I have been slowly climbing further up the mountain each time I make this trip. I have no idea the route I will take, although I have set my eventual goal on making it to the top of the Anthill, that bump on the side of Thousand Lake Mountain as seen from Bicknell.

From town, you cannot see the top of the mountain. Drive a few miles west and suddenly you become humbled. The mountain just keeps rising and rising until it looms as a colossus dwarfing the Anthill and everything else, everything but its neighbor, Boulder Mountain.

Its neighbor, but once its same self, layer on layer of continuous rocks. Repeat the litany—Moenkopi, Wingate, Kayenta, Navajo, Carmel, Morrison, Mancos—and finally the basalt cap. Both mountains are level on top, both at about the same elevation, both capped by the basaltic lava, but the underlying layers don't match.

This is where it gets interesting and complicated. A major geologic fault opened and separated Boulder Mountain from Thousand Lake Mountain. The latter side rose. And rose and rose, pushing itself up slowly and deliberately, careful not to fold or warp anything. If I could have sat here at that far distant time, I would have

risen like Aladdin sitting on his magic carpet. Then, after
another vast amount of time, they both lost some rock
to erosion. Sitting higher in elevation, Thousand Lake
Mountain shed more of its softer layers of rock, such as
the Mancos Shale. Then, when they were at a similar
elevation again, but still high above the desert to the
east, lava flowed from cracks in the ground in a glowing
and spreading lake. When it cooled, it put a solid and
protective cap on the surface. End result? Everything else
looks normal, except the type of rock I'm sitting on here is
hundreds of feet higher than my imaginary doppelganger
sitting on the same type of rock of Boulder Mountain.

I find myself right smack in the middle of one of the
most awesome spectacles and histories of this earth.
Most people don't notice things like this. Of course the
geologist does, but the people living in the village below
me don't know and most of them don't care. They look at
the mountain every day of their life, they see the red rocks
and the white rocks and the black rocks, the trees and the
deer. They don't need to know any more than that. If they
go explore in the woods, they are trying to shoot an elk or
a deer, or catch a fish, or track down a wandering cow.

What I like about this place where I sit is there are no
cows, and no signs of people, at least not recent people.
The place I picked to sit and catch my breath and eat my
apple does show signs of people. Anasazi, or Fremont, I
don't know the difference, but the spirits do. I have just
discovered a petroglyph panel that as far as I know has
never been discovered by anyone else in modern times.
This is the middle of nowhere that is only a mile from
somewhere. But it's a tortuous route to get here and there
is no reason for anyone to come here, certainly not to
find a cow or elk or deer or to fish. Can't ride a horse here
and I can't see anyone walking for the fun of it. Except

me. I call this fun? You bet; I am sitting in my own little corner of heaven.

What are these carvings doing here, though? Someone else obviously was here sometime in the past, well before there was a name Thousand Lake Mountain, or Wingate formation, or Wayne County, or United States of America. A time in the past, just like the rocks of the past. The feeling I have of sitting here looking at this vast panorama, then looking at the rock carvings is one that I think some religions call bliss. I am in awe, a part of history. Think about it.

I see spread out above and below me that history lesson of rock. The red rock that was a boundless horizon of red sand dunes at one time, then white sand dunes, meandering rivers, mudflats. Then swamps where dinosaurs walked and dodged the falling ash from distant volcanoes, replaced by endless oceans and mud drizzling onto the seafloor to depths of not just feet, but thousands of feet. Then bright blue sky again hovering above earthquakes and the gentle rising of the very earth itself. Finally wind and rain that started tearing it all down again topped off by the latest burp of lava that coated the landscape like a black layer of snow. And a time span of millions upon millions of years.

Then the people came up here for some reason. What was it? I will never know, nor will anyone else, except the spirits of this mountain. As I look along the cliff, I keep finding a new carving. There is a bighorn sheep, next to a snake. And the handprints, they keep showing up. Is this rock art doodling? Is there a history lesson here? Is it a sacred writing, or a message to the spirits, or maybe a map of the area? Why is it here in this specific place where there is no water anywhere near, and the climb to get here—wow. Why here I ask, this time aloud, not to myself but to the spirits that I know are listening.

I'm glad they are here, untouched, unmarred by some saint's name. Elijah, 1879 or something similar seems to be pioneer graffiti all around this country. Elijah never made it up here. I did, so I just sit and listen. I am blinded by red—the rocks, the sand, the pink clouds as they reflect millions of acres of red slickrock desert east of me. The breeze cools me as I reflect, rustling the pinyon and juniper. It etches circles in the sand as the ricegrass twirls in the wind. It blows ceaselessly as it has since this rock was formed from this very sand, pressed itself into rock, then slept for millions of years. Now it has seen the sunlight again, and the rain and wind is tearing it down.

That is part of the message I see in front of me. The circle of life is a sacred belief of the indigenous peoples. We are born from the earth, it nourishes us, we return to the earth. Well, there is a circle of the earth as well. The rocks erode over millennia of endless rains and wind, the sands are formed into rock once again, they are blown over vast deserts, then are carried grain by grain over eons of time to the seas. The seas dry up, the land moves and heaves and floats over the face of the earth, the rocks are exposed, the winds and rain go to work again, the grains of sand start to fall down the mountain and start another journey to the sea. How many cycles over how many eons?

And I listen to the wind. It seems so harmless, so soothing, so never ending. Did the artist of these cliffs sit here and listen to this same wind? What did he or she think about? Are these carvings his message to the gods? Did she find awe and wonderment and inspiration from the same spectacle I see now? The endless winds and rain have since muted the carvings, protected though they are by an overhang in the cliff. Erosion continues, sand grain by sand grain as the wind works patiently with no concern other than to undo what has been done before.

It's bad enough that I try to understand just the geology of this place. Now I get into the human history of it and the mystery of our comprehension of all this. Just listen to the wind. It is a mantra in itself. The pinyon jay doesn't worry about all this, he just looks for food.

I need to think about how much further I will go. It is still a long climb to the Anthill. I've just about gone the distance of the level part. It starts uphill from here, and my legs are rubber now. I think this is my limit for today. Maybe next time, I can take it another phase farther. I will have to leave the red rock and go upward onto the white. The black boulders start showing up just above me. Why aren't any black rocks here? Why is it everything has a question? This trip is starting to wear me down mentally. Physical exhaustion from a hiking exploration is explainable, mental exhaustion is a little more difficult to understand.

This country does it to you, though. Nothing is simple here, at least not for me, not today. Maybe next Saturday I can come up here and just enjoy the warmth, the sunshine, the fantastic scenery. Maybe I will find a new petroglyph panel and just look at it and say, "wow, look at the carvings of sheep and snakes."

I get up and put on my pack. It's downhill from here. I carefully tiptoe my way across the sand. I really don't want to step on the cryptogams. I can follow my earlier footsteps, but why take the same path; I've seen all that before. I come to the edge of the plateau. Where is my route down through the Wingate? I think back on what the Wingate is, a marvelous winding wall of red sandstone snaking through southern Utah, throwing a challenge to road builders and pioneers alike. One goes for miles sometimes either above or below the cliffs to find a precipitous route through. Certainly no road possible here, but it is climbable. That is a rarity too. I've found two different places just outside town where I can get through the Wingate. If I do nothing else in this life, that is a worthy accomplishment.

I look down at the civilization below me. In the valley is the other world I live in, the highways, the town, the people. I leave my red wilderness and ask my last question. What is for supper tonight? I can deal with questions like that.

OCTOBER STORM

I sit once again among the jumble of slickrock boulders and ledges, blue sky overhead, red sand and juniper creating a labyrinth of amazement for me. The cliff is a hundred yards to my right, diving off into the depths of space and time that are the Canyonlands. I sat here six months earlier, musing about space and time that this vision pulled me into. I longed to return, as I will long 'til the end of my days.

It seems I am drawn here like iron filings are drawn to a magnet. I belong, but no one really belongs in this place. Maybe my old friends the raven and the chickadee belong, but they can live in three dimensions. I can belong to only two, if that. But those are physical dimensions, not spiritual. I don't know how many dimensions there are spiritually. And spiritual is what I have to be talking about here. For me, the hidden dimension of time seems to explode into my consciousness, overwhelming all other senses. This is a place about time more than the red rocks, the twisted juniper skeletons or the expanse of empty space. I realize the space below me and past the cliffs is not really empty. It is filled with time, invisible but overpowering.

My wife and I drove over to my private Mecca yesterday, hoping to enjoy an autumn time of solitude and rest. A time to sit in this very spot and reflect on this view, trying to make sense of something that is well beyond my poor ability to make sense of. It is that time of year when the cottonwoods pierce the bluebird sky with the seasonal supernova of color. The eye piercing brilliance burns a hole in the sky as well as a longing in your very soul. It is a time of endings, when the autumn prepares us all for the annual death rituals and soul searching questions.

We happened instead onto a rare treat. Rather than a sun filled sky, we were enveloped in one filled with rain. It was pouring as we drove into Moab. Red water ran alongside the highways. Slickrock hillsides glistened like an ocean suspended on end. Blue black clouds hid the red rock cliffs. Air was water. Clouds feathered down from the dark mass trying to escape. They were twisted and shredded, touching the ground, then swirling up to disappear, then rearranging themselves, all the while releasing torrents of rain. This was not the summer thunderstorm short-lived-fury type of rain, but that of a late autumn cold front, dragging with it a sky full of Pacific Ocean.

As we drove through Moab, heading south to our secret place, blue sky and flittering peekaboo sunlight shafted through the clouds. Ever moving, ever changing, as if nature was reasserting that whatever attempts all the divergent forms of life were making, the basic fury of physics and chemistry still could overpower and awe anything in its path. Not unlike the wars going on in the cosmic sky, featuring galaxies and exploding nova and devouring monsters called black holes. The black clouds consuming the western horizon were a tamed down version of a cosmic black hole as they headed towards us. The little teases of blue sky disappeared into the racing fury of ocean water escaping its brief air born life. It was in a hurry to return to the anonymous comfort of the sea a thousand miles away.

The fury of the storm soon passed, more bluff than bluster. But it reminded me why I was here. I was drawn to the raw power of the earth, the elemental forces of wind and rain, time and space. The relentless rains and wind I just witnessed, expanded over the millennia of autumns and springs, are the patient forces that created this desert. Time, in infinite expanses that are as unknowable to me as I am to the raven riding the currents that define his world.

This rocky piece of earth is indeed a magnet to me. The storm clouds, soon to be racing over the Great Plains far east of here in a different world, drew me here. The rocks, in their slow melt from cliffs to boulders to sand, show a patience and an irresistible force that is as inevitable as the sun falling from a desert sky. Watch as closely as I can, I cannot see the change. But as surely as the magnet rearranges the iron atoms, the force of this place pulls on my soul in an unseen pattern. It will continue to pull me back here, just as it has drawn my soul in some unknown previous reincarnations.

The sun is out today, the day after the storm. I sit nested in the sandstone boulders to shelter myself from the cold north wind. The storm may have passed, but its western edge still pushes the wind. I must wait another day before I get my peaceful solitude of a warm October day.

But the force that flexed its power is the force that draws me here. I cannot live long enough to see the change as it happens, but I look out past the cliff's edge, to the infinite void below me. That is the result. It is an overpowering nothingness that is the result of millions of years of storm and wind, chickadee and dinosaur, sunlight and melting ice. Time. The time expressed in a raindrop, a gust of wind, a grain of sand.

A raven rises on a thermal, appearing above the nearby cliff, then soars overhead. He doesn't care about time or space. He simply enjoys it for what it is. It is an unbridled enjoyment of life. Why cannot I do the same?

Interlude:
Clouds of Heaven

Twenty thousand feet below lies Utah.
Northern Utah, where the cliffs and mesas are brown,
Not the red orange slickrock desert 200 miles south.

I see clouds ahead of us.
Not a few puffy blobs, but a wall.
August monsoons hiding an approaching
     Wasatch wall more solid.

Peek a boo outliers soon hide the mesas and the brown.
A break just in time to see the Green River snaking below.
Not green; barely lined with green in this lonely desert.

We dodge and maneuver, flying between canyons.
Not the rock canyons of the land, but white canyons
     of cloud cliffs.
Oh the clouds!

Walls of immense billowing puff pillows
Intense white edged and contoured with deep blue.
We weave between cottonball walls, hiding mysteries
     in their white mass.

Surreal, as if a hallucination in three dimensions
     explodes all around,
Stalagmites below, expanding towers above.
A fantasy of floating sculptures.

Rising above and falling below, thousands of feet
    in every direction.
Walls of misty air with no boundary.
We magically pass them by but do not enter
    their mysteries.

Gravity has disappeared. We float in animation.
Entranced, my face presses on the window.
Space passes but not time. I have entered eternity.

I yearn to leave the confines of the airplane.
I want to float between the clouds, not in them.
Surfing the edges, caressing the bulges, rounded
sensuous bumps and curves.

No longer able to fly looking in,
We enter the fog of cloud.
The magic fades into mist.

We disappear.
The world is gone.
Space turns white, time ends.

I close my eyes.
I do not want to leave the cloud,
Unless to wander its edges forever.

Is this a metaphor for life?
The boundaries hold the magic.
The substance is a misty illusion

Interlude:
Spring Thunder

Exploding greenness.
A child of a wet winter and warmness of a late spring.
Savor the green of April and May.
Soon it turns to desert brown in the baking
    dryness of June.

Look for surprises each day; the first iris this week,
    strawberry last.
We anxiously await buttercups down on the creek.
Then wild geraniums, columbines, claret cup cactus.
It's a riot of color, a riot of life.

Today thunderheads are building, a preview of the
    monsoons of August.
Blackness and rolling thunder to the west over
    Surface Creek.
The black clouds missed us again, Cedaredge is drenched.
Maybe next time we will feel the rain.

I watch for lightning. It is far off.
At first cloud to cloud, then a ragged jagged finger
    stabbing the ground.
My eyes anticipate the flash, hard to focus
    on where it lands.
It comes closer, faint at first, then louder.

The thunder reverberates through the canyons,
　　rumbles over valleys.
A boom echoes for minutes. The sound waves bounce
　　a hundred times.
Rock to rock, tree to tree; nature's grand symphony.
　　It goes on forever.
It is not noise. It is a concert of passion.

I look into the valley spread beneath me.
The pink and white blooming orchards disappear.
The curtain of cloud drops to the ground.
Grey, then blue, a mist ere sunlight returns
　　as stairs to heaven.

Darkness marches from the West, but Land's End is
　　still in sunlight.
Glistening white glows from snowy peaks.
It is still winter there, and will be for weeks to come.
The hummingbirds hover here in watchful wait.

Winter is passing, spring arriving.
Tell the snowflakes that as they struggle to land,
　　but melt in a cold rain.
Green overpowers the last assault of cold.
We wait, thankful for winter's sleep, anxious for
　　the heartbeat of spring.

SEASHORE

To see a World in a Grain of Sand,
And a Heaven in a Wild Flower,
Hold Infinity in the palm of your hand,
And Eternity in an hour.

~ William Blake, *Auguries of Innocence* ~

Bodega Head

Bodega Head. The name evokes a wild world full of adventure and mystery. That is what I see before me now. I don't know my Spanish well enough to remember the meaning, though I'm sure one quick peek in the dictionary will inform me. I knew it once, but sometimes a little uncertainty and ignorance can be refreshing. Right now I don't want to know. Bodega Head. It rolls off the tongue with a hint of strength and power, like the white spray of surf below me. I'm on top of the head with the feet and knobby knees of this headland far below. From that frothy, thundering edge, the Pacific spreads west to forever.

No sandy beach here. No peaceful reflective moment watching the sands shift up then down. The waves break hundreds of feet off shore, pushing further until flattening with an avenue of foam, then welling up for the final effort, bouncing, crashing in an explosion of spray over the jagged black rocks. These spires and triangles of battered polished rock thrust above the water, the final survivors of a long eroded cliff. They dare the surf in an effort of futility. They seem to stand firm in their epic battle, but the determination of the waves as they charge, then erupt in shattered defiance, is heroic and successful in the end.

Between the outliers of rock and the edge of the
continent, where I sit like an eagle (or, more aptly, a
watchful seagull), is the churning confused cauldron of
white and green, a grinder, a translucent pulverizer. How
can anything survive in that maelstrom?

Quite a lot it seems. A seal head has been bobbing here
and there, content in his chaotic world. He, or she, is at
home, confident in the ability to play and chase food and
avoid sharks in the calm and not so calm spots. There is an
entire world under the waves I cannot see or comprehend.
The rock down to my left is covered with birds—black,
upright, resting between flights. When the surf retreats,
as it will by tonight, the symphony of life in the tidal pools
will astound me, but not the seal. As with the chickadee in
the desert, this is home. Any other form of life is unknown.
The seal and the cormorants don't sit and wonder about
how it can be otherwise, like I do. They know nothing else.
How peaceful can that be?

I am a stranger to the sea; more importantly I am a
stranger to the seashore. The sea itself, today, is peaceful
like its name. The seashore is as pacific as it gets. There is
no wind, no recent or approaching storm. The November
sun is warm as it dries the dew on the green-and red-tinged
ice plants at my feet. Ever since time began, the sea has met
the shore in a continued struggle for dominance. The sea
has always won, for that is where land begins and ends.

I wonder when someone else previously stopped
here, next to where I sit, and found their own peace. An
unknown person has carefully picked an assortment of
wildflowers, tied them lovingly with an old shoelace as
a bouquet, and placed it by the edge of the cliff. Is this a
memorial, a tribute to where a loved one flew off the edge?
It would be a quick way to end whatever plagued them. A
quick fall to the rocks, the pounding surf, the edge of an

endless sea. Or was it a memorial to a lost love, placed where they once stood in starry eyed bliss long, long ago? Or perhaps it was someone who loved the sea and this is where their eyes and mind were filled with the sea in all its philosophical glory. The possibilities intrigue me, but this gesture had powerful meanings. I will respect the feelings that now live here, placed by someone unknown to me and the cliff.

Whether or not the churning sea below swallowed a life or simply symbolized the freedom of boundless eternity, it is in a turbulent peace with itself. I want to think the water exploding off the rocks has traveled across a world. I know it hasn't. The water below me, in foam or spray or sandy green motion is the same water, replenished only by the droplets of fog or showers of winter rain that has been swirling around for years. The wave is what has traveled. And what is a wave? The wave moves, but the wave has no substance. It is the energy of the earth, the very cosmos. It is that force we will never grasp, never comprehend. It is as old as the earth and was once part of the very stars that have come and gone, just as this cliff has come and gone—many times.

I am looking down on time itself. The scene below me could be today or a million or a billion years ago. There is no progress, no advancement. The combination of sea meeting land does not come and go like the civilizations of the Nile or Babylon or the Indus Valley. The dinosaurs have walked this very same scene, as did upright apes who walked until they could go no further. You could say their very species walked off the edge into the swirling maelstrom that enveloped them.

And the thought that a similar scene is playing out right now on another planet of another sun of another galaxy, well, that fills me with even more awe

and wonder. It puts the bouquet of flowers in a whole
different perspective. Of all the time this cliff has stood,
and the times other cliffs in other places have endured
the thundering of the surf, where else has one sentient
being picked flowers and grieved a lost soul? We have the
capacity to love and understand, to respect and honor. The
force that can move a wave across the oceans cannot think
and show such emotion as this. No wave, no rock, no seal
or sea gull has yet to show that. If we can do that, how can
we do harm to the other forces, the other lives we share
this ocean and land with? And by chance we are able to do
harm, we are destined to soon erode into sand just like this
solid cliff.

STINSON BEACH

As I sat on the rocky shore of Stinson Beach one afternoon when the fog lay a few hundred yards offshore, I recalled a time long ago. The thunder of the waves uncovered memories buried as deeply as the driftwood in the sand. During my college days, it was one of my first exposures to the seashore. Christmastime visiting my future bride, I showed off by throwing rocks at seagulls along Stinson Beach. Now, decades later, I sat on the sand where the beach ended at rock cliffs. Humbled by the ocean, I was more than humbled by the idea that I could put into words anything not already thought, if not written in prose or verse, by human minds over countless millennia. That was a stretch of time that reached as far as the gray green seas stretched to the horizon, still shrouded in the mystery of fog.

The waves were as ceaseless and cyclic as time itself. They never stopped. They came in thundering breakers, like the winds over desert sands. Was the tide coming in or going out? If I paid attention, I could tell. But I was paralyzed by the hypnotic rhythm. In and out. Crashing, then pausing, as if to look around at this strange phenomenon called land. Then retreating, as if satisfied there was no more sea to float on. Then back to the anonymous comfort of the sea.

The gulls were further down the beach. I couldn't hear them anyway; the roar and thunder of the sea was all consuming. It called to me. It called to the very bedrock that lay jumbled on the shore, now slowly turning to

polished sand, unconcerned about fog and sunsets. Time
ends on land as it does with the foamy waves.

Once, these very rocks, black and green, serpentine or
olivine, a metamorphic mélange, crashed into the continent
after riding the seafloor waves from somewhere west of
here. Ages so far back, creatures that no longer exist on
this earth roamed the shore. Time so remote, the very sea
that brought the land here no longer exists. What I saw
was something new, unknown in that long ago world. That
thought humbled me more than even the ocean itself did.

The sun tried to erode the fog as the sand eroded the
boulders on the shore. It broke through, bounced off the
horizon of water, then sank behind the fog. It was a cycle,
what I saw that afternoon. The sun powers it all, the water
resting after its trip to the sky, an interlude as fog and
clouds, then a wild ride back to the sea as rain. The rocks
formed under this sea, took their own wild ride to shore,
rose to the sky and now await the rain and wind and
endless sea to fade into sand. Sand which will turn once
again to rock, the water which will float back to the sky;
the sun heats it all. And we come to the sea to think and to
write and to try and make any sense.

I could make no sense, nor did I think anyone had
before me. A lot had tried. Some spent their lives, certainly
more than my meager hour staring in hypnotic wonder.
I could float out on the waves, circle the earth, pound
seashores for the millennia I dreamed of, and come
back with no more idea than I had. Maybe there was no
meaning. The waves roll in and roll out in a never ending
search.

The sun broke through, although dimmed by haze. I
saw the white line marking the fog out there, away from
the jumble of land and cliff. Go beyond the breakers
and the sea was calm, rippled and sparkling with sunlit

diamonds. It did not beckon me as it had so many others throughout time. Where I sat at its edge, that's what beckoned me. I like edges. Forest edges, river edges, canyon edges. Now the sea edge. I wanted to know what ends and what begins, sort of like life itself. I wanted to know what was there before it started and after it ends. The pelican skimming the line of waves didn't care that anything more than fish under the surface were calling to him. I couldn't be that content. The tide was coming in. But wait awhile and it would go out again. It was as ceaseless as the answers I would always seek. They were in the waves. They were the waves.

MUIR WOODS

I am nestled in a hollow at the base of a middle-aged redwood tree, sitting on a forest floor padded by brown needles and twigs. It is cool, of course, and a grove of furrow-barked giants towers all around me. I am not alone, but it is as much as I could achieve here today. I had to get away from the people. Crowds of visitors walk the paved thoroughfare down below me, gawking straight up and snapping pictures, none of which will show anything other than the fact Uncle Harry was here. You can buy a bumper sticker proving that. These people don't belong here. What pushed me to the brink was a fat man strolling along talking on his cell phone. He certainly is wasting his and the trees' time.

If he doesn't belong, do I? As a species, probably not. So many places we do not belong, but we are here, in teeming numbers, not understanding, destructive in our arrogance and ignorance.

I knew if I hiked off the main trail, onto a lesser one, then off of that one to this grove, still too close to the few hikers still adventurous enough to climb the steep trail above me, I could get a better feel for the sacredness of this place. Voices still carry, but what are they saying? And why are they talking so loudly in this sacred apse? Where is the awe, the respect, the courtesy to these woods? "Be quiet and listen!!" I silently scream.

Hear the fog droplets falling off the needles one hundred feet above. Listen to the creek tinkling down the needle-padded and rocky draw. Feel the torrent rushing

down here during the January floods. What else uprooted
and toppled this young giant to my right? It is peaceful
now, but peace is not what shaped this valley. Flood and
wind and other furies shape this as they shape me. When
we understand all this, then we can belong and we can
hike here in droves.

Can I upgrade my citizenship from homo sapiens to
sequoia sempervirens so I can belong to a species that has
proven its ability to belong? My current one has proven it
doesn't have the responsibility to belong to such a noble
place as this grove, this peninsula, this planet. To survive,
yes. To belong, well that means we fit in, are accepted; we
can live in harmony. The redwoods do. They signify the
majesty of their creation; they tower in dignity, their green
tops climbing to their heaven. Hidden in the deep shade of
noon, dabbles of sunlight speckle their heads, an occasional
spot of sunlight brightens the ferns on the hillside. They
move, but not as much as I would like, my being used to the
transient ways of humans. Maybe I could get used to their
pace. My curiosity could be satisfied by quiet reflection, by
cool breezes off the nearby ocean. I could climb higher and
higher, maybe catching a hazy glimpse of the sea, where
someday, smoothed and weathered by waves and sand,
a branch or root or even my entire long body might float,
settling eventually back on land.

I could drop dead needles like fingernail clippings. I
could shelter the owls and seagulls and countless others,
feathered and furred. I could share gossip with my sleepy
neighbors. I would talk about much more important things
than these noisy humans, chattering nonsense as they
plod along the trail, disturbing the peace, the quiet. We
could compare the blue of the sky with the white trilliums
far below, carpeting the ground. We could talk about the

deer creating her own trail, wondering if she smells the salty air. Laughing that my head is in the sun while the squirrels down below are peering through the fog. We could point to the rays of fog, reaching tendrils of silver past our tall trunks as the heat of midday lifts the cloud back out to sea.

But then, if I were a tree, I would miss the human things—the writings of Steinbeck, the symphonies of Mozart. I would not hear the questions of Socrates or see the sculptures of Michelangelo. I would not feel the courage of Lincoln or guess the aspirations of Jefferson. So, as a human, I am doomed to dream of the dark forest floor and peer at the dots of blue sky far above the green ceiling of the forest. I am not a redwood, at least for now. Maybe next time. So, like an uninvited guest, I stand outside, looking in, pretending I do belong. I look up and smile with a wish, a longing to be asked to come in. I appreciate the cool respite from the heat far above. I bask in the filtered sunlight, sensing the energy that flows upward from the moist, deep soil, inching upwards to the needles far above. Ferns dot the hillside, as do the laurel and moss. The water that has escaped from the thirsty roots surfaces to babble down the stream, seeking in its relentless search the endless ocean nearby. I cannot hear the roar of waves meeting the shore, but I know it's there. That's for another day.

The crows are dancing in the blue above the treetops, breaking the stillness by their raucous laughter. I think it may be the same language as the silent redwoods, but it's too loud for me. I prefer the quiet.

It is time to go. The hikers above me are noisier than the crows. I can feel the unease of the trees. They want their quiet. I do too. I can move on, trying to escape the crowds. The trees have the patience to endure. The patience I will gain when I can make that transition to sempervirens. Will I remember what it was like to be so hasty and mobile? Maybe I won't miss it.

• • • • • • • • •

After penning my thoughts, I had no more than climbed back up to the trail when I met a white haired man who said something I could not understand. French, I think. He turned and pointed uphill and mumbled, "Wild animal." I looked, smiled and said, "A deer." He said, "Ah yes, deer." I thanked him and walked on. It was a doe being followed by three forked bucks. Ah yes, indeed. I thought we were the wild animals. The deer were simply doing what they do. It is November and the rut is on. The boys, they simply do what they have for millennia. Doing what my species has done so well, it had me sitting wishing I were a tree. We bred ourselves out of any understanding of what exactly we have done. But then, we aren't the only ones. I watched the bucks pursue the doe, noses high in the air, pulling in that irresistible scent. Then I sat in a thicket of young redwood saplings. Way too thick. Only one in a hundred will survive to make it to their sunlight sniffing height. Most will die, before reaching the size they can and should. The deer realize that, as do the adults of the sempervirens species. They talk the same language. Can I learn it in time?

Interlude:
Laughingwater

It flows and gurgles as it tumbles down,
Encased by green edges,
Sheltered from the world.

Sparkles of sunlight undulate on the water,
The outside heaven searches into the shade.

Listen as water gathers from countless seeps and springs.
Collecting strength and courage,
It announces its goal.

Jumbled rocks temporarily block the path,
But the force rolls on, seeking the sea
So far away.

Listen to the murmur, the burble, the splash.
It falls, flows and fumes
Breaking free to find its way down.

Over rock, under branch, through the tangle,
White, brown, green, transparent as it moves.

It caresses the green velvet of the moss
Clinging on the rock, just above the flow.
Falling, then pausing, then continuing on.

Stair steps of motion,
Racing, running, hiding, escaping,
It cannot be stopped.

Listen to the birds, laughing in tune to the flow,
They are hidden,
Searching their own world.

They flit and hop, fly and bounce through the glade,
Rarely seen, but always heard.
They guard their tunnel of shade.

The distant whoo of the dove,
The whirring twitter of the hidden wren,
The steady melody of the grosbeak.

Close your eyes as you stand in the stream,
Watercress at your feet.
The water, the birds, the rocks, the trees,
All are calling you.

Listen to the laughter, feel the life giving grace.
Become the peace as it journeys on
To an unknown place.

It is life itself passing you by,
Becoming part of you, then gone.
It is ever searching, ever moving.

Then it reaches its end, to start over again.
Sheltered from the world,
It is the world.

Interlude:
A Water Journey

I float in a vast azure sea,
Watching whales below and albatross above.
One caresses me with waves and froth.
One sails through me as I drift skyward.

Released from former bonds, a new self.
I search for companions to coalesce.
We gather, seeking diaphanous adventure.
Swirling, billowing, rising with the tropical heat.

Perched above others, I am blinded by the rising sun.
Turning pink and orange, and fire red,
We grasp the winds, racing higher than the heavens,
And start our eastward journey.

I gather with others, a formidable army,
We march to an unseen coast, unfamiliar worlds.
Our adventure turns to a rumble, full of lightning
    and thunder.
We jostle in violent circles.

Many newfound friends turn to ice and fall,
    lost in the depths.
I gather new friends as we continue a race to the shore,
    over the mountains.
Circling in a giant dance,
Swaying in rhythm to our own symphony of wind
    and thunder.

Soaring peaks below reach up to squeeze us,
    push us upwards,
Now turned to ice, we fall, drift, helpless in the wind.
I melt, freeze, melt, reform as a magical snowflake,
Out of the maelstrom of wind, now in free fall, silent,
    a work of art.

The ride is over, peace has come.
A new ocean of white, blanketing the mountains.
I sleep, frozen, buried.
Waiting, waiting.

Faint light above me slowly turns brighter.
Blue, then white, but I burrow deeper, now liquid again.
I feel free, I can move and flow.
As the light turns brilliant yellow, I have dug into
    the warm soil.

I crawl past hard pebbles, past grasping roots.
I hear the parched call of filaments, surging with
    my neighbors.
Pulled into the plant, I gurgle upward.
A green blood, I bring nutrients to countless cells.

They sigh relief, sing praises, pull sunlight, brightening
    my form.
Unknown to me, flowers form, life creates life, seeds
mature.
I am pushed out a leaf, vapor again, weightless.
As over the ocean, I float upward but find no cloud.

I drift in the new sea of blue, past trees, past meadows.
The brilliant sun disappears, blackness of night chills me.
I merge with the ground, gently on a grass leaf,
Forming as dew, glistening in the glow from the rising sun.

I vibrate as a giant form pounds the ground near me.
The bull elk mouth envelops the grass, my dewdrop.
I start a new journey, down a hot, dark, tube.
I mix with the digesting grass, a nutrient cocktail.

Now part of the red blood, coursing through veins
     and arteries,
Forming meat, muscle, the elk himself.
I wander the forest for years
Until I am dropped in a grassy sea.

Fellow droplets fall as a gentle rain,
Picking me up for our long journey home.
Through rocks, down a rushing stream,
Long, long miles, jostling, resting.

At long last, we enter the sea,
Our salty home, lost in depths unknown
Resting, floating, sinking, drifting.
Awaiting the day I find a new journey.

FAUNA

*One does not meet oneself until
one catches the reflection from an eye
other than human.*

~ Loren Eiseley, *The Unexpected Universe* ~

ASSEMBLY OF ANGELS

M arch sailed in again with the annual flight of
sandhill cranes. They filled the spring sky like angels with
outstretched wings, dangling legs, red eyebrows, and a
sky-filled chorus of honks and clattering crane beaks.

Winter was difficult this year, with spring slow in
coming and snow still blanketing the lowest slopes of the
nearby mountains. I started seeing the migrating birds
a few days earlier as they flew high overhead, filling the
air with far off honks. The thrill of finding the tiny dots
of gray was part of my rite of spring. When the sun was
right, it would catch the stroke of wings flashing white like
celestial strobe lights. Since they had been arriving daily,
I felt it my duty to drive the few miles and welcome the
visitors as they landed for an overnight rest. I stood along
the highway next to Fruitgrowers Reservoir, reliable as a rest
stop on their annual migration to the breeding grounds of
prairie and tundra far over the northern horizon.

Just as I arrived, the dotted mass of distant cranes
coming from the south started to fill the skies. I looked
into the gray of the thin cloud cover masking the
spring blue of the Colorado sky. They came in scattered
formations, flight after flight. Hundreds. How can anyone
tell how many? A guess. Perhaps even thousands, as thick

as the swarm of gnats hovering over my head.

They filled the sky in a swirling, circling mass. Some
so high they were only specks, lower masses turning
and crossing with the groups higher, lower, intersecting
but separated by hundreds of feet. A moving sculpture,
three-dimensional from my two dimensional viewpoint.
Looking up, it was dizzying. They flapped their wings, they
soared, they turned, circled, and passed by, a confusing
maelstrom of flight. They weren't landing yet. They were
reacquainting themselves with this familiar rest stop, a
larger lake this year than usual. Tomorrow they would
be gone again. Today had been a long flight. They flexed,
rested, and stretched tired wings for the descent. Airborne
for how many hours, how many days? More days would
pass before home would be reached in a far off world, still
mottled with snow.

The crane-filled sky, moving, pulsating with birds high
and low, was a spiritual experience, but overshadowed by
the noise. Thousands of crane throats proclaimed their
exhaustion, their thrill, and their excitement of being
alive and on the move. They exhibited the pure instinct
thousands if not millions of years in the perfecting. How
do you describe the songs of angels? Honking, clattering,
chattering; a deafening chorus in all directions. I wanted
to dance and join in the magic. What were they saying?
Compared to the song of the meadowlark or the wren
or towhee, it was grating noise. But it was their song,
understood only by themselves, and it was pure joy.
How could one stand by the reservoir on a March day,
surrounded in all directions by the large, lumbering
birds dancing in the sky, proclaiming their dominance in
sight and sound, and not feel surrounded by God and her
retinue of attending angels?

Wave after wave, the formations came from the

south, reminding me of the movies of the Great War. The
prisoners of Europe could not have been more overjoyed
seeing the hundreds of allied bombers covering the skies
over Germany. They came and they came, filling the sky.
The flapping wings of my imaginary bombers stopped
as the flying changed to the soaring of rigid wingspans.
Soaring became a circling descent. Heads raised from
their horizontal postures they had held unceasingly for
hours. Feet, serving on the long flight as trailing rudders,
dangled suddenly. The birds dropped from the sky,
prehistoric looking, like pterodactyls. They fell like some
awkward, gangling contraption. They circled to earth,
then on final approach, feet forward, wings outstretched
and flapping, they landed with a running touchdown.
Finally, hours after they last stood on earth, they stopped.
They stood, mingled, and shook themselves like wet dogs.
They preened tired wings. They looked around. Some
stood, some walked. Some made a graceful glide as they
searched the ground for morsels of protein for nourishment.
Some strode in a purposeful strut, adjusting themselves
to a slightly different location. Maybe they didn't like the
company they found themselves in. Maybe they just wanted
to stretch those long legs. They milled around like a herd
of sheep. Some, in graceful courtship, faced their mate, or
possibly their rival, and jumped straight up in the air as did
their partner, wings outstretched. Then, when the dance
was done, they stood with heads straight up, opened their
long beaks, and filled the air with their passion.

The noise had now moved from the sky overhead to the
fields below. Stragglers still flew in, still circled, and now
had to decide where to land on the crane-filled lakeshore.
Ducks skittered on the water, jostling for position. Geese
honked in annoyed disturbance from the thousands of big
visitors. Two muskrats swam contentedly by the roadside,

unperturbed by the convention going on around them. They beeped as they swam by, then dove in a noisy disappearance under a ripple of water. Two deer grazed on the sagebrush hillside, oblivious to any change in their world.

The gracefulness of the flying birds, disturbed only briefly by the comical descent to earth, now assumed the regal stance of their earthly presence. They were large, surprisingly large with that overabundance of feathers. The long wings tucked against the body had too many feathers to store without looking like some fan dancer who grabbed two boas instead of one and now had to try and store them without lessening her flustered dignity. The movement on the ground didn't stop, just as the skyward movement still flowed with ease. But here, close up, you could see the majesty of the whole bird. The red eye patch colored the otherwise drab gray brown of the huge body.

I was exhausted by emotion, by the thrill of watching the assembly arrive. It was another day to the flocks, one day of many in transit. One day in the ages old drama of moving north, to be followed months later by the return trip, to be followed next year by the same journey. It was as old as the mountains and as dependable as life itself. I thought of the migrations that don't happen anymore. The passenger pigeons once blackened the sky. The shaggy bison flowed on the plains like a river that ran from horizon to horizon. The salmon turned the forest-shrouded rivers of the Northwest into foaming, churning highways. Too many of our fellow beings are now gone. If one passage of a day's flight of cranes could inspire the awe I felt, what could I feel from the millions of travelers now gone forever?

It was then I understood what the cranes were saying. They were talking to me and to all my kind. It was a defiant laugh. We, who didn't understand, who didn't care, also didn't belong. I wanted to join them tomorrow and fly north to the endless plains. I flapped my arms but I couldn't fly. I apologized to them and to those who have gone before and will never return. I closed my eyes and still heard the call of the cranes. It was a chorus of angels. I bowed a silent tribute, then said goodbye.

JORNADA OF THE RAVENS

Does the shortest day of the year upset the behavior of beings other than humans? Lack of sunlight does affect the sanity of people who live in northern climes. It even has a medical name, SAD or seasonal affective disorder. But does it affect birds? Ravens for instance.

Driving down off western Colorado's Grand Mesa on December 20, just hours before the winter solstice, my wife and I witnessed a jornada, or journey, of ravens. A determined passage of hundreds of ravens stretching beyond human sight. We were entranced by the view of the Gunnison River valley below us, including the snowy expanse of jagged peaks of the San Juan Mountains to the south, when my wife noticed ravens flying north in formation. We see this occasionally from our house, only a few miles distant (as the raven flies) from this spot. They fly over us from the valley to somewhere else higher up, and then they fly back again later in the day. Sometimes they stop and circle over us, harassing any golden eagles in their way as they casually make their journey. This reoccurring event usually involves up to fifty ravens and only happens in the winter.

But this undulating flow of black wings and bodies involved more ravens than I had seen in my entire life. They stretched below us in a stream as far as we could see, appearing to come from the hazy depths of the Black Canyon of the Gunnison. We had to stop the truck and pull off the nearly deserted highway to watch. We were playing a tape of Mannheim Steamroller Christmas music, listening to the throbbing and powerful beat of the Little

Drummer Boy. The music fit the scene perfectly. It was a grandeur to all senses. The sight, even without the birds, was an expanse of majesty. The oncoming stream of birds, flowing from the horizon, was awe-inspiring. The music added the right tempo and accompaniment to the flight. As we sat on the lonely road, watching the procession, I looked behind me and saw the object of their intent. The oakbrush-capped knoll behind and above us was black speckled with ravens. They were landing on one acre of land, creating a carpet of glistening black dots, hopping and jostling as a velvety, moving apparition.

Where were these birds coming from in such a large number? I could understand a flock of geese, or more often in this area, sandhill cranes, although they would be either months earlier or months later than the end of December. But ravens? They live here. They don't migrate. But obviously this day, this most sun-starved day of the year, they were journeying to somewhere from somewhere else. Were they climbing the mountain to search for more sunlight?

As the music reached its inspiring crescendo, I pulsed in tune with the flapping of the wings. An intense flapping that signaled exhaustion, in need of rest from a long flight. The column continued to come from the south in a glorious and mysterious continuity. They just kept coming. And they just kept filling the knoll behind us.

Suddenly the column to the south swerved in unison to some unknown field of energy in their path. The birds, even those a mile or two distant to the south, swerved as one. They turned west, then circled, then continued on their original path above us. I looked behind and the knoll was empty. Either they were frightened off, or this was just a resting place after all on a journey to a further goal.

Finally, the column thinned out and then gradually

ended as the last straggler brought up the rear. The jornada
was over, at least for now. I thought about comparisons
with humans and how we move and migrate and flap to the
trends of the times. How a landscape like this in our modern
West attracts our species in columns like these ravens. We
come and come and fill the view with our presence.

But then, I threw that thought out of my mind. Let
it pass unhindered like the ravens. I was watching birds
and who knows what they were thinking. They were
consistent and determined. They knew their goal and they
were achieving it. They were moving as one, leaving little
impact. Maybe they were affected by the winter solstice
and maybe not. It didn't matter. Their jornada passed in
magnificent indifference to the humans below. The human
journey is ongoing.

THE LAST GRIZZLY

What does the last grizzly in Colorado think as she ambles along a September lakeshore hidden in a maze of spruce forests and wildflower meadows? Or does she think of anything other than finding a meal? She long ago quit thinking of finding a mate. I say she, since that makes this story more poignant. It could be a he, but he probably would long ago have left the area, to be shot by some myopic hunter mistaking a grizzly for a deer or coyote.

An old trapper told me a few years ago he saw a grizzly recently in Colorado. I silently discounted his claim while nodding in politeness. Claims of grizzlies in the state are abundant enough to fill a book. Officially, the last grizzly died thirty years ago in the headwaters of the Conejos River. As a wildlife biologist myself, I am not now so sure.

Especially after today, when I was shown a plaster cast made of a bear print that, if not a grizzly, is the biggest black bear in the Rockies. I will not reveal the exact location, since the person who sat in front of my wood stove on a rainy December day did not tell me. I knew, though, it was near the sighting made by that old trapper years ago. The endless miles of gently rolling spruce forest broken by repetitious lakes and meadows certainly can lose a person. They can hide a grizzly as well. After seeing the tracks and photographs, I had few doubts in my mind it could be a grizzly. An old, lonely grizzly who has wandered in isolation for decades. The experts will probably say it is a huge black bear, but I prefer to think otherwise. The size of the tracks is off the scale for black bears. The 29 inch stride for the walking bear who made over two inch deep tracks in soft dirt makes the weight close to 800 pounds. It doesn't matter whether or not it is a grizzly. That it's possible is provocative.

Wildlife do not read textbooks. They do not eat and behave as we predict nor live where we tell them. Their intelligence surpasses ours, even if they can't do exponential equations. We discount our own intelligence when we think they are dumb. Just ask this old grizzly still wandering her lonely world.

But that is my dilemma. I wish I could ask her a few things. I want to know if she realizes she is all that is left, at least in these mountains. She and her kind ruled the forest and meadows as well as the prairies and valleys. We killed them off with ruthless arrogance. Defeated rulers sometimes lose their humility. I want her to be defiant, but I doubt she is either humble or defiant. She is just there, imparting wisdom we choose not to hear.

I know we are not supposed to anthropomorphize. Sorry, I can't help it. I cannot apologize to her, although we all should. She is out there alone and there will be no more when she is gone. A union of one does not pass on DNA. And she is too far removed to meet up with the few grizzlies left up north. Wolves may be heading our way, but I don't hold my breath for griz.

So, what does she think? She doesn't know the days when she could wander further down the mountain, cleaning up buffalo carcasses on the plains. She doesn't know that once upon a time, her ancestors saw only an occasional Ute, not the hordes of ATV's, four wheel drives, and exploding metal sticks killing everything in sight. Does she even know there should be more like her? She must remember her mother, who raised her with a fierce protectiveness. Those carefree days are over. Now she is the last. Alone.

Setting aside the photo of the massive bear print, I looked out at the gray rain obliterating the mountains. She is out there, curled up in a den she has relied on for decades. Will she come out next spring? Will it be her last? What do I say one summer when I go out to ask her my questions and she is gone? I will look at a forest that lived with griz but now knows an eerie silence. I will never see her ghostly shadow disappearing into the mist of a gray rain. It is I who is very humble. It is I and my kind who are lonely.

WHEN THE HUMMINGBIRDS LEAVE

I can set my calendar when the hummingbirds bring spring with them. At my location, I count on April 21, give or take a day or two, to welcome the first hummer. Often it is just a whirr of wings as the first outrider whizzes by, maybe stopping, maybe just teasing me with his passing shadow. But I have anxiously awaited them, food ready in the feeders, to announce another season.

Usually, the lazuli buntings are fast behind, and a little later, the black headed grosbeaks, Bullock's orioles, nighthawks, and other migrants. But I don't await the first ones of these. They are part of the crowd that pushes out the winter birds, such as the juncos, and brighten late spring and summer with their jostling, filling the air with joyful noise. But they don't have the meaning, the anticipation of the little whirlwinds.

Within a week or two of the outriders, the lagging main entourage arrives, mostly black-chinned, but a few broad-tailed. The males lead the way, choosing their territories, awaiting their mates. Whether they have already chosen or do their courting at their new summer home, I don't know. I do know they put on their displays of diving, circling high, buzzing down, hovering, and intimidating for several weeks. How they avoid crashing into branches, buildings, the ground, I will never understand, but they have been perfecting this display for eons.

Often, they will have to huddle down, shivering, wet, during a late spring snowstorm that often slams into us in early May, but they survive. There is nothing more dismal than an otherwise perky, vibrating hummer braving out these snowy interruptions, dripping wet and sitting on a branch. But I have never seen a dead one. However, I have only found one nest in years of looking, so they are also good at hiding.

As the days lengthen and nesting begins, I am entertained by dozens of hummingbirds flitting, bouncing back and forth, and jostling for feeder position. I have tried to count them, but it is like counting a swarm of mosquitos. How many are there? I guess two dozen, but there is no way to count. Easier to count electrons vibrating in an atom.

Sometime in July the rufouses arrive from their northern breeding grounds. They are bronze, have a metallic whir, and make me want to swat them with a fly swatter. Much more territorial than my docile black chins, they drive off others from the feeders and then sit regally in their arrogance. I keep telling them there is plenty of food. In one large feeder is more food than he can consume in a lifetime, but still he drives everyone else off.

Then in August, I notice a thinning of the crowd. Still a crowd and still a daily chore to make food and fill the feeders, but something has changed. Unlike the finches, jays, grosbeaks, and others, I cannot tell the young hummers. But I am sure many of my whirring friends are the young of the year and the parents have already started leaving. The dry heat of June is gone and the thunderstorms of July and August have brought relief, but all of a sudden there is something in the air that hints of autumn. A slight breeze, a cooler evening, the sun slinking further south. I finally notice the hummingbirds are fewer. By September, we are not making much food. I change from large feeders to much smaller ones. A few leaves are hinting yellow. The Maximillian sunflowers are showing yellow.

Then the shock hits. I saw only one hummingbird

today. Then two days with nothing. Then one more. We approach the equinox and I wait. No one. They are gone. I said my silent goodbye a week ago to the two still hanging around. I wished them well and godspeed. I hope they get past the powerful storm bringing remnants of a Pacific hurricane our way. Snow has already dusted the highest peaks like powdered sugar.

I leave the feeder up for at least a week after I have seen the last hummingbird. I stare at the unused feeder hoping one last migrant will stop on her way south. The feeder seems so forlorn, so lonely. It matches my feeling. I know they will be back, but the feeder is ready to end another summer, as I am ready to end another one as well. I am at the age now when it is possible I could not make it to April. I brush off the thought, but some day, it will happen. For now, I will just think that I have spent another summer communing with the cheerful bouncy hummingbirds and will look forward to another one in seven more months. Endings do not always precede beginnings. Sometimes, endings are just that.

There is no one date to end the season as there was in April. I think their arrival is spread over a couple weeks, but their departure is spread over a month or more. I cannot know these details. I don't know if they know themselves, but somehow they make it work.

Like a permanent resident in a vacation resort town, I now feel the loneliness of their departure. I am left to survive the winter, the cold, the snow. I will not be alone. My winter friends, the juncos, the chickadees, the deer, will all show up more often to keep me company. But I do feel the silence; I miss the bouncing and whirring back and forth, up and down, their cheerful little beeps and twitters. I smile when I think that as I stare out at the first big snowfall, there are people far to the south who are now enjoying my hummers. "Take care of them and send them my way," I think. A much anticipated day will come with the arrival of the hummingbirds next April. I will be watching the calendar.

But for now, I will clean the feeders, put them in the root cellar, wait for the juncos to return, say goodbye to the golden aspen as their leaves twirl to the ground, bring in the firewood, and await the long, cold, dark days until the winter solstice. Then, I will look at the new calendar and count the days until April 21.

Interlude:
Buttercup Part 1
Big Cat

A warm January afternoon;
melting snow and singing birds.
Cattail down drifting on the breeze,
clouds of a coming storm gathering above.

I stood on the edge of the creek,
the calm shattered by Goldberry barking,
lunging forward, retreating, fur raised
looking to me for help, a look of panic.

My mind raced back in time.
One month ago, almost in this very spot,
I found fresh tracks of a big cat.
Puma, the stealthy stalker of the forest night.

Goldberry cornered her in a thicket.
I grabbed the dog, pulled her away,
waiting for the scream, the spring, the leap.
It didn't come, but I felt the spirit lurking
        silently in the forest.

A hidden visitor to this catly paradise,
roaming secretly, never seen.
Abundant deer for nourishing meals,
a secluded spot to hide and hunt.

Now, once again, I waited for the attack.
The cat lay tensed for her leap,
first for the dog, then maybe for me.
I held Goldberry, then planned my defense.

But the leap never came.
The body lay still,
never to move again.
Head cocked backward, tail straight.

Life was gone
from one that lived on other lives.
I edged forward, carefully, cautiously, catlike,
with respect, with awe.

A scream lay silenced in her mouth.
Searching eyes closed,
powerful feet padded black, claws hidden,
outstretched tail no more to balance the leap.

Deer can rest safely now,
although they never do.
Maybe her grown kittens and grandkittens
will take her place.

The deer need the cat as much as the cat needs them.
We need each other in this amoral life.
Fear balances beauty,
food balances fear.

I stood in silent tribute,
richer for her being there,
thanking her for avoiding me.
Thanking her for my fear.

Death takes us all,
sometimes by force, sometimes in sleep.
Sleep may have taken her.
A peaceful end to a violent life.

But violence for her?
No, part of life that struggled day to day.
One day merging to the next,
hunger balanced by meat just often enough.

She symbolized power, stealth, surprise.
She lived in grace and ran with the wind.
Her tail swung in symphonic rhythm;
her eyes caught every movement.

Until now. She missed the movement of my hand
to touch her massive paw.
I stroked the tail, caressed her fur
with reverence, respect, and awe.

Her death brought a meaning of life to me,
a thanking of the force above us all.
I have sensed the power of God—
her god and mine, the same.

Rest now, forever, in these hills
until we meet again, your power and mine.
You have gone to greet your god,
I have glimpsed a shadow of mine.

BUTTERCUP PART 2
THE NAMING

We named her Buttercup.
She lay at the edge of a small meadow
filled with yellow buttercups in the spring,
now months off, forgotten in the snow.

We came down the hill today to say goodbye.
She has lain there, secretly, for maybe a month,
a mystery death, a sad ending,
but one we all face.

She was a mountain lion, cougar, puma, catamount.
Pick the name, they all look the same.
The long tail stretched in a line,
head twisted in that final look back.

Not understanding what threw her down,
not foreseeing as we do
the everpresent stalking of our own end.
Doing what she always did, but always was such
      a short time.

We stood in respect, in reverence, in silence.
A warm day, melting snow still on her back,
the tan fur glistening with beads of water,
      dripping to the ground,
nourished now with lion energy to feed the buttercups
      when they awaken.

The deer die from old age, from lions themselves.
The birds fall from the sky, mice in traps, unwanted.
The big ones, the meat eaters, the hunters,
We don't expect the death for them.

They kill, they are not killed.
When the mighty fall, it shakes our faith.
I saw the halo of her god on the fur, in her claws.
It renewed my belief.

Life goes on, nourished by death.
Buttercup will live on, in the springtime yellow
     of her garden.
The startled ears of the deer as they sniff the air,
will announce her spirit as it stalks the snow.

She would have snarled at the thought
of such emotions she never knew.
Her task was to eat, to live, to prowl the darkness.
Hers was the movement of grace in the night breeze.

You still live, Buttercup, in the frozen December stars,
hunting with Orion, unseen, unforgotten.
Knowing you are there, I respect the night,
I watch the deer; they respect you, too.

BUTTERCUP PART 3
THE DEPARTURE

They came today to take her away.
Two uniformed officers, young, men of nature.
They needed to find out what felled her,
    this young lion.

The wildlife officer visited the other day
to view the body, to answer the riddle.
The metal detector showed no bullets.
He had no other answers.

A later call said he needed the body.
The state vet said plague was a possibility.
Big Cats were dying in Wyoming,
and could be here, too.

The plague. A word of fear.
He knew I wanted her left here, but I said yes.
We need to know, but not for her.
We need to know for the rest of us.

That god I saw—I didn't want to meet just yet.
Buttercup had met hers, she is no longer here.
So I said goodbye, I stood in tribute once again.
Let them come. The spirit of Buttercup lives here now.

They trod down the hill,
and tied her to a pole.
A drop of blood fell from her nose;
she swung as they walked, primitive hunters
    carrying their prize.

I smiled through the sadness.
It was victory for her.
Her magnificence spoke through the silence.
It was a march of honor through the snow.

They will cut and test and probe her
thoroughly for the secrets.
But she and I already know,
whatever they find matters no more.

She lived and she died,
as do we all.
If not by plague, then by another force.
Does it matter in the end?

We all will depart in sorrow,
carried by some stranger.
Looking for answers
that may never come.

Interlude:
The First Sunflower

Today, the first sunflower of the season opened.
Not the domestic, eat and spit the seeds type.
The real thing, wild, from time immemorial,
Independent and free, as we all wish we were.

Yellow, bright, vibrant, eager to follow the sun.
Petals reaching out as a sunburst,
Center, dark as the earth, the factory of life.
Green leaves, scraggly, eaten by grasshoppers.

I could sit all day and watch it twist and turn
As it follows the sun, from northeast to northwest.
Like a child chasing a butterfly,
Its hope organic optimism.

Unlike its domestic cousin, with one huge solitary flower,
These have an array of flowers up and down the stem.
As soon as one has fulfilled its life purpose, another opens.
I think it knows how popular it will be.

First, the butterflies, white, black, red,
And combinations of all the above.
They flitter by, realize the promise,
Then circle back and land.

Crawling around in the cornucopia of food,
They suck up the nectar and pollen,
Then lumber off to land and absorb the feast.
Soon, they are back for more wonderful gluttony.

The bees and wasps dart and hover,
A hummingbird explores, backs up, bounces around,
Then returns to the familiar sugar water of a feeder.
Easier pickins there, I guess, but he still looked happy.

As the seed ripens, the flower locks into a final position.
One day I notice it doesn't turn any more.
It doesn't greet the sun, it doesn't seek
        the noontime high.
Its job is done, it rests now.

Petals wither, petals fall.
The flute song of the flower turns to the bass drum
        of the seeds.
They fatten, mature, then call the birds.
A new phase begins.

The finches and sparrows, chickadees and nuthatches.
They send out the message: seeds are ripe.
I worry no seeds will fall to hide in the winter soil,
But enough do. They have to. It is nature's way.

This is why the sunflower exists.
Why the butterfly lives,
Why the goldfinch nests.
Life is a circle, a golden web of sugars and nourishment.

The sun chasing flower is a byproduct.
They brighten my summer
And entertain my autumn.
My spring is an anticipation of
    green new plants to do it again.

Interlude:
The Butterfly Migration

The migration had begun.
First one, then another, then several.
Soon, hundreds of Painted Ladies flew past.

Floating, bouncing, gliding, they flittered and fluttered
In a steady stream from southwest to northeast.
They came up the hill, dancing and darting between trees.

They were small.
They were determined.
They ignored me sitting in wonder and
    fascination with their flight.

They were going to a safe place only they knew.
How many miles had they come, how many to go?
I tried to ask, but they wafted and bounced past
    alone in their world.

Some kept flying, some stopped to sit on a branch or rock.
They would fold, then unfold wings.
Brilliant colors exposed, red, black and orange.

I compared them to the birds they were flying past.
The lightning speed of the hummingbirds, the majestic
    soaring of the eagles.
My awe of avian skills did not match my admiration
    of the butterfly flight.

There was no grace of movement, but it worked.
It was a perfection of a type I still looked for.
It was the courage of a small heart
    and the determination of fragile beauty.

They continued on in their quest.
I watched as the stragglers bounced and fluttered
    along their unmarked path.
Then they were gone.

Places

*Climb the mountains and get their good tidings.
Nature's peace will flow into you as sunshine flows
into trees. The winds will blow their own
freshness into you, and the storms their energy,
while cares will drop off like autumn leaves.*

~ John Muir, *Our National Parks* ~

HOMESTAKE MINE

The August evening was hot and sultry, not untypical for the Black Hills of South Dakota. About a dozen of us had gathered to tour the famous Homestake Mine of Lead. Originally started by George Hearst of the famed and wealthy Hearst family, the mine now was the centerpiece of the Lead area. The underground portion of the mine delved deeper into the earth than any other mine in the western hemisphere. We were to descend over 5,000 feet to nearly sea level. The open pit portion of the mine on the surface was starting to eat the town of Lead.

A fellow employee at the Spearfish Forest Service office, whose significant other worked at the mine, had arranged this private tour—a five hour personalized glimpse of a different world. My wife and I jumped at the chance. I was still new to the Hills and found this opportunity to explore the world beneath our feet exciting.

After a mine official gave us a safety lecture, we were outfitted with hard hats, headlamps, and carbon monoxide monitors. Then we all crowded into a large freight elevator and started the descent. Since the lowest depth was over a mile below us, it took several different elevators and short hikes to get there. I lost track of statistics and details, but the mine was huge. It snaked around for what seemed like miles following the veins of ore. The natural darkness was pitted by strings of incandescent lights lining the walls. I felt like Frodo groping along the mines of Moria.

The rock was not even granite, but a metamorphic rock of melted sedimentary rock, either sandstone or limestone. This fractured and ancient rock was riddled with veins, which along with some of the metamorphic rock itself, was infused with tiny bits of gold, silver and other minerals.

The temperature increased with our descent. We passed one level filled with giant earth moving equipment. The guide said this was the garage area. The vehicles were taken apart on the surface and then ferried piece by piece down to various levels, where they were then reassembled to do their heavy work. I was impressed at the herculean effort to blast and move rock in this hadean depth.

We ended our descent at the lowest level, where no mining activity was happening. Mine officials were pondering how to improve the air conditioning so men could work here. No one pulled out a thermometer, but my senses said it was well over 100 degrees. The humidity was obvious, with water seeping out of numerous fissures in the walls of the cavern and draining to pits where huge pumps sent the water a mile straight up to the surface. They were still finding gold in the veins, but the cost was increasing to the break-even point. Go a thousand miles west and we would be at the sea shore watching waves move microscopic bits of gold in with each wave. It was amazing what humans would do to get this golden colored bit of earth. It was everywhere on Earth, but only economical to mine in a few places. This was one place, but until people were willing to pay a few dollars more for that piece of jewelry or Canadian Maple Leaf coin, we might soon be seeing the end of the burrowing here.

As our guide was talking, I was looking at the rocks, rubbing my hands along the hot wall of rock. I leaned over to pick up a small piece of quartz. No one told me to put it back, so I assumed it was just that—a piece of quartz from 5000 feet beneath a surface covered with ponderosa pine and bluestem grass. This was not a diamond mine where we would have every orifice in our bodies searched when we left. If we wanted to cart out plain rock, then we were welcome to it. In fact, one inch diameter core samples were given to us as souvenirs when we left.

We were all getting quite uncomfortable from the heat and humidity as was our guide. We all now knew as much as we wanted for that night so we started the long ride and walk up to the surface.

Not until we resurfaced and all headed back to our cool and dry homes did I really start to understand what we had seen. As we drove through the pine and aspen forest in the moonlit darkness, I said to my wife that no way would I ever buy anything made of gold again. She agreed. The mining industry was literally moving mountains to gain small pieces of a golden metal. Why? Gold has been treasured and sought after for millennia. It has been the measure of wealth which was the measure of success of kings, queens, and would-be's. Civilizations have been overpowered and slaughtered to gain gold and silver.

We had seen beneath the surface of the magical land known as Paha Sapa—the Black Hills. Somehow I felt like we had violated mother earth by looking inside her. Her private inner being was just that—hers and hers alone. We had seen something no mortal had ever seen until recent times. Seeing a cliff or the belched lava from a volcano gave hints, but we had seen the inner sanctum, a man made intrusion into the depths of our sacred mother.

We returned via Spearfish Canyon, beside a streambed

which was now a dry rocky swath. It was diverted near
its headwaters miles to our south to feed the thirst of the
Homestake Mine and the town of Lead which serviced
that mine. That stream had flowed for millennia, carving
into the limestone that now stood as towering cliffs lining
the canyon. This was the same limestone that was carved
by nature into magnificent caves further south, Jewel
and Wind, both National Parks. This was limestone that
hid beneath the surface of the pine, aspen, and paper
birch, which then hid the elk, deer and porcupine. This
was limestone that once covered the massive gneiss of
Homestake, now upthrust along with the granitic mass of
Mt. Rushmore and Crazy Horse to the south.

The Black Hills were and still are sacred to not only
the Lakota but also to other tribes who once roamed here.
When Columbus and Magellan were sailing unknown
oceans, people hunted bison and prayed to their gods and
spirits that roamed this vast prairie. I felt the sacred energy
as well as I roamed the hills and grasslands of this bubble
of rock rising from the plains.

The moonlight cast shadows, never seen by the rock
deep under the mine's entrance shaft. Standing a mile
deep, there was no way to understand the spirits that
lived among the pine. You never felt the summer breeze
or spring thunderstorms. You never heard the bugle of the
elk in a golden-leafed autumn. You couldn't have felt the
thunder of the seas of bison running with the wind. No
one could hear that anymore, no one except the spirits of
Lakota, Absaroka, Cheyenne and Arapaho. I wondered if
their spirits ever searched deep underground for flecks of
golden nuggets. They valued other things more important
to them, such as an eagle feather, a bison horn, and a
grizzly claw.

The more I thought about the wonders of the Hills, the

more I found the depths of the rock ugly. That rock was not sterile, but it was lifeless. Once upon a time, it was deposited in a very life-rich sea. But its glory days were over. Life on the surface continued on, unaware of a billion years ago, when there were no bison or pine.

The Lakota saw life as a circle, a cycle of wind and rain, birth and death. The rock of the Black Hills will cycle into grains of sand and will seek the far off sea.

But it will take more lifetimes than any of us can measure. Even more than the spirits of Lakota and Cheyenne will see. The rock that now rests a mile deep may eventually surface again, but the specks of gold will wash into a sea that will see them as just another grain of sand. There will be no one to pull it out and wear it on a finger.

As we left the canyon on the outskirts of town, I heard an owl calling in the distance. He didn't care about mines or gold. He was only looking for a rabbit. Life was much simpler when our ancestors were more concerned about finding food than digging deep for yellow rocks. Historians can call it progress, but I doubt if the owl agrees. Progress to him is living one more day, one more spring.

WEATHERED DREAMS 1980

It was built in the summer of 1882. Never mind the reason, nor even the names of pioneers who spent the many weeks of back wrenching labor. We will never know, so why ask? It served the purpose of sheltering its inhabitants from the questioning of the wind and the confessionals of the relentless blizzards. By '95, it was abandoned. Left to decay, to silently entrust its story to the meadow, which was slowly engulfing it in its web of evolution.

I stand here now by myself, eighty years later. It is nearly November and the snows have yet to arrive. It is that expectant time of year when the taunting warmth of the October sky teases one into a sense of foreboding anticipation. The wind is only a hint of itself, waving the brown and dried meadow grass into a uniform, rippling sea. The breakers crash onto the shore of fir and huckleberry. The cabin sits as a shipwreck on a shoal, never to reach the shelter of the forest, the safety of its protective cover.

The wind and sun have etched a pattern of grey and brown in the ancient grain of the logs. Remnants of a forest long since burned and decayed are now surviving as meadow mice and chickadees, buttercups and snowflakes. Why do I wish to view through its eyes its lonely history? It is a continuous replay of snows and winds, summer storms, blue skies, and elk passing by in solemn apathy. Yet it appeals to me as can no Broadway play, Chicago museum, or work of Plato, Shakespeare, or Jack London. It has not the freedom of the hawk nor power of the wolf.

The beauty of each log was long ago shattered by an axe. The shaded earth of its floor cannot grow even a blade of grass.

I try and listen for the silent dreams. I hear the echoes of a thousand years. The wind creates its own symphony, with backing from a chorus of creatures feathered and furred. Even the sunlight seems to vibrate as it fights through the floating strands of clouds.

The weathered old cabin stands here in tribute to forgotten dreams because it exists in a harsh world, miles from the world defeated and rearranged by me and my kind. It offers treasures such as an unbroken sea of grass, meadow mice, chickadees, and a wind that sings only to a mind that can understand.

Leaning Cabin

This was the year for me to discover old cabins. I had marveled at the old weathered cabin not long before I found another lonely, isolated cabin miles away. It also was built in a world that no longer exists. By people who are now dust and atoms circling the earth. But the cabin stands. It is leaning as if trying to lie down to rest, tired from a century of wind and blizzard, lightning and rain. As we all get, it is tired, but as we all endure, it struggles to maintain its existence.

It sits in a lonely meadow, far from the nearest road, unknown by all but a few hunters and hardy hikers who happened this way as I did today. It is shown on no map and owned by no one but the encroaching aspen forest, now sending up new green sprouts at the cabin's edge. I think it appropriate. It was cut from a forest long burned or dead, but is being reclaimed by the descendants of that forest. Sort of like from dust to dust. From tree to sprout.

Life is about change. We all change, we adapt, we evolve. The old prospector, hunter, trapper, deluded optimist of a homesteader, whoever built it, has long gone. Also blown away in the winds of a hundred winters were the dreams and hopes that drove him to exert the back breaking effort to build this small cabin.

Did he mean it to lean? Was he so tired that when he stopped to rest and lean on his double bitted axe, he was at an angle that tilted his world? Maybe the back logs have rotted first and the cabin is settling, as I tend to settle into the old easy chair after a hard day of work.

There is no road nor even a faint trace of a wheel

track within a mile. How did he get the stovepipe and the glass window up here? I can hear the complaint of the mule team that pulled a wagon through the forest and across the meadow, head high in grass and wildflowers. This was still primeval country back in those days. As I said, it was a different world, with different dreams. A world waiting to be tamed, conquered, subdued. In many places, it was. But not here. The elk bugles his haunting melody in the autumn wind. The chickadees still rule the forest, overseen by the hunting goshawk. Someone drew a line on a map and penned the words "official wilderness," but that only shows the ignorance and arrogance that we can mandate something as natural as a grass covered meadow, a forest of aspen struggling to survive in a stand of emerging spruce.

Nature takes care of her own. The forest will survive wind and fire and beetles. The meadow will shift from here to there, but knows to feed the elk somehow. The chipmunks make do with whatever they find. The owls take care of the fertile mice. It is a circle and a cycle and it turns without our help.

And the cabin will lean even further until one lightning filled July night, it will crash to the ground and be embalmed quietly and reverently by the sunflowers and gentians and timothy grass. Then the aspen will cover it all with golden leaves as they whirl and twirl and swirl to the ground before that first October blizzard. Then the snow will hide it while the voles and moles burrow their tunnels, mixing everything together. The spring will call all life and continue as if the cabin were never there. And soon, it will never have been there. And that is all as it should be.

LANCE CREEK, WYOMING

I reach my favorite highway, Wyoming Route 270, which leaves US 18 at Manville and heads north to Lance Creek, then east to rejoin US 18. It is not really a shortcut; it is a lesser highway that avoids Lusk and, more importantly, avoids much chance of the Highway Patrol. Wyoming roads should be traveled at over 70 mph, and that's risky to do on US 18. Maybe I feel more like an eagle going that fast. Wyoming should be seen through eagles' eyes. Besides, the feel of this highway is much different than on US 18.

I turn on AM 680, KOAQ, Scottsbluff-Gehring. Golden Oldies, tunes that evoke a feeling of something lost. I will always think of the 60's as a Renaissance of music, a time equivalent to the creative Florence of Michelangelo and Leonardo. It is an explosion of melodies and songs by a mélange of groups and individuals not seen since. A time of hope, frustration, and idealism that will not be seen again in my lifetime. The music set the mood of something great, a time of excitement, anticipation, and slowly fading memories and broken dreams.

As I look at the land flying by me, I sense the same broken dreams. The same feeling as times gone by for many different people, a time of sadness, anger, faded memories of greatness which very few recognize, much less appreciate now.

I see it as I come over a rise south of Lance Creek. White limestone cliffs define the rise and border a row of trees in an expanse of grass and sky. This is Wyoming. Some call this view desolate, no sign for miles indicating man has ever set foot here. But look closer. As I drive on, there is an occasional sign that someone did try to tame this expanse. Civilization tried to gain a foothold, but lost— an old cabin, a pair of wheel tracks going to the horizon, and of course, the highway.

The thought occurs to me that this is symbolic of the struggle of white man. This was the home of the Cheyenne and Lakota and who knows how many others for millennia before them. This was buffalo country. Remove the highway and the power line, the shack, remnants of old windmills, and the few scattered cows. Remove the old side road that vainly leads to a hidden ranch. "Hepp Herefords," the sign says, is somewhere over the horizon. Off to the right sits a rusted old yellow tractor, sitting by itself, with nothing else near it, saying, "what am I doing here?"

It doesn't belong, but once, there were people who did belong. There were people who lived here, albeit as nomads, passing through, always moving. They knew the land and were a part of it. They had a tragic struggle and they lost.

Red Cloud, Spotted Tail, the Lakota, the Cheyenne, broken treaties and meaningless promises. Whites came and said they had a better use for the land. The proud people who lived here for millennia were reduced to beggars, leaving few signs. Those early pioneers who destroyed the red man's dreams left signs of their own broken dreams. Yellow tractors and windmills are here, but where are the people now? Houses do not belong, nor do power lines and cows.

In any economic sense, it is a wasteland—scabby hills, sagebrush arroyos, exposed red and white rocks. The highway is actually quite scenic now, lined like a boulevard with yellow sweet clover covering the right of way, stopping at the fence line. There, sagebrush and grass take over, stopping only at the horizon. Off in the distance stand a few lonely cottonwoods.

Modern man does not belong here. This is quite evident, to me at least; he does not belong, but he is still holding stubbornly on. Ahead in the distance, I see the community of Lance Creek. How did it get its name? Sounds kind of romantic. Was it some battle? Did they find a ceremonial lance, dropped by a Cheyenne warrior, maybe from a Sun Dance? Surely there were some cottonwoods then, just as there are now. Does anyone living in Lance Creek today understand what a sun dance even was and how it was significant to the people then?

The sky is painted a somber tone, like the country itself. It is early June, no thunderstorms building like there will be a month from now, but there are speckled clouds which often precede early spring rains. Clouds that are full of hope and promise, which is soon shattered since the rain doesn't make it to earth. It is virga, which evaporates along with the hope of rain.

In this country, you really do rejoice with rain. It is a tough country, but everything that grows here does belong. The ground soaks up the rain and relinquishes it to those things that appreciate it. No waste here, the country is very forgiving in a way, but very unforgiving in another way. It is most unforgiving to those who don't understand the way it is supposed to be. That is why no one lived here permanently before the pioneers arrived. The Cheyenne didn't build houses or fences or windmills. They passed through, taking what they could and giving back what they could, then they moved on. The people did this, but so did the bison and the eagle.

It will return to that someday, but only when no one tries to live here permanently. How long will it take?

Small communities will slowly die, a future of much of the West. Manville is almost a ghost town, Lance Creek is hanging on, but only by a dirt-filled fingernail. Once these families are gone, will they be replaced? Will their children stay here to face a lonely, harsh and frustrating struggle, destined to lose eventually? Will anyone else come to go through the struggle these folks and their parents went through to make any kind of decent living?

I look forward to the day when the bison are back running free. And they will be someday. More than anything else, this magnificent beast symbolizes to me what this country is about. Slowly, yet oh so surely, they will return.

Lance Creek. Population: 175. Elevation: 4600. I slow down as I enter the town—a country store, which doesn't look very lively, the Conoco Station, a tavern with the ever present Coors sign. Coors Beer: another symbol of the west. It once belonged to the west, but it has lost its innocence and has covered the nation like an epidemic. Coors was Golden, it was the Colorado Rockies. It was the first beer I ever tasted—at Kulagi's on the Hill in Boulder. Even Coors has lost its meaning and its place in the West. I pass the Post Office, lonely all by itself. It says Lance Creek, Wyoming. The Zip code starts with an 8, but I space out on the rest. I space out on Lance Creek. It is gone as quickly as it came.

Someone just did the first cutting of hay along the right of way, lying there in rows ready to be baled. Where you put water, things will grow, stop the water and the sage soon takes over. We don't cut sage, it is just there.

I come around the curve on the edge of Lance Creek. The line of cottonwoods defines the creek, or what is left of the creek. They stretch off into the distance, seeming like they could go on forever. The road leaves the creek and now, once again, I am surrounded by the vast expanse of grassland, arroyos, and lonely barren hillsides. Once again, I am reminded I do not belong here.

The music grabs my attention. The great old songs had lyrics you could understand. That is one reason this road has meaning for me. You combine the oldies played on this radio station with this scenery, its history, and it is magic. It does go back. It is more and more an ancient past now, a time when the music represented a whole different world than we have now, a time of my youth, and hope and anticipation and dreams. Maybe that's the music that evokes the feeling that the Cheyenne and Lakota had—the good times. The times when we were young, a time when we felt we belonged. The world was there for us.

To me, it is the music of the 60's. To someone a little older, it could be the music of Glen Miller, evoking a similar feeling of times when their world was young and hope was challenged by a world gone crazy. I suppose we all have our Golden Oldies. I really do think mine is special, but don't we all? To the Cheyenne of three hundred years ago, the sound of drums, flutes, and chants of warriors could evoke that same feeling. Maybe it can be any kind of music. Music is a gift of the gods. We need to listen carefully.

Recently I read about a big dinosaur find in the country over the horizon to the north. That is really going back in time. Can anyone comprehend a million years? I think about dinosaurs and science and the struggle we must face with those who doubt even such things as a million years. Science itself—the very facts of our existence and ancestors—is being challenged. That mentality drove off the Lakota, ignored their heritage and now ignores our meager role in the grand scheme of things. That mentality seems to still hang on in places like this.

But I wander. Come back to today. Things are cyclic, and maybe we wander in and out of history, repeating ourselves, learning lessons only to forget them. What difference is there between the dinosaur and the Cheyenne? Is our loss any different than that of the wooly mammoth who roamed here a blink ago?

Thoughts are getting too philosophical. A badger crosses the road in front of me. He has no philosophical dilemmas. He is just there, like the sagebrush, a symbol of the toughness of this country, a symbol of something gone but still tenaciously hanging on.

The power of the music slowly fades away, like the Lakota of old. A time gone by, never to return. I see the main highway up ahead. Like a time traveler, I brace for my return to reality. But what is real? It is I, wending my way home along a desolate prairie.

Reality is what we make of it. It is this road and KOAQ, waiting for me to drive this stretch again. Perhaps it will be on a snowy day in December, with the winds of Wyoming howling across a prairie, in search of bison, and dinosaurs.

Interlude: Dragonfly

The July sun beat down without mercy.
Air baked in 90 something heat.
I threaded my way through dried grass and cactus flowers
To the pond at the bottom of the hill.

The air cooled as I welcomed the gurgling creek.
It flowed clear and cold, spring fed, in its own world.
A small decades old dam, plastic lined by me
Now served as my storage for lawn water.

Pumped to the top of the hill
To transfer some of its life giving wonder
      to my flower beds,
It kept enough of its energy here
To transfer me back in time.

The dragonfly darted from cattail to cattail.
King of the pond, he sat in quiet anticipation.
Wings outspread, white and black striped,
Unchanged since he flew swamps
      before dinosaurs prowled.

Darting around him were countless blue damselflies,
Wings folded, transparent,
Much smaller and as delicate as a silk embroidery,
They added grace to his powerful presence.

Water striders skimmed the pond,
Casting spotted shadows on the silt and moss bottom.
A small frog leaped into the shade of the watercress.
A pencil thin garter snake slithered across the surface.

I stood surveying the setting.
It could have been millions of years before.
A forest of cattails towered above me, covering
    the small flat.
Their prehistoric flowers spewed yellow pollen
    in the breeze.

A song sparrow in the trees above me warbled his song.
Hidden, he brushed aside the heat with his aria.
Calling to whomever wished to hear him,
He brought a smile to my face.

I scooped algae out of the pond,
Stirring mud and silt that turned crystal clear water
    to brown soup.
The spider webs disappeared as I swept the surface
    of the water.
"I'm sorry," I said, but I knew they would
    be back in minutes.

The brown of the hillside watched enviously
    the green of the stream.
How many shades of green?
The light green of the cattails, darker of the watercress,
Deep emerald of the algae and moss.

On this day, the blue of the sky was one tint,
Washed out in the heat and haze.
But the greens, spotted with darting dragons and
    damsels, blues and blacks,
Gave the backdrop to the steady murmur
    of the clear water.

The silt I stirred was now settling,
Creating swirls and folds in the water.
Wait a few more minutes, and my presence
    here would disappear.
Only my footprints in the mud would disturb the pond.

My mission done, I stood in thought before I started uphill.
The sounds were of peace and calm, burbling, buzzing.
The smells were primordial ooze, fresh and swampy.
The greens of water plants cooled the air.

The water was now clear again, water bugs active.
A bubble rose from the bottom, bringing silt
    up in a mushroom burp.
The water flowed on, as it ever does.
A dragonfly flew a circle, then landed again, black
    and white wings outstretched.

INTERLUDE:
THE WEATHER STATION

The old box lay in a garage, neglected,
Tossed aside like an old rag.
I'd been searching years for one.
The Weather Service said, take it. Surplus to us.

I loaded it into my truck, took it home,
Rescued like an abandoned dog.
It would sit now near my yard.
Giving shelter from the sun for my thermometer.

The slatted box once housed an older thermometer
Sitting in some remote meadow.
Helping a young agency tell someone who cared,
A history of temperatures, highs and lows.

White paint peeling, boards warped.
Rusted screws and nails, some loose.
The metal tag says "US Weather Bureau,"
Long ago renamed the National Weather Service.

What does this shelter know, where has it been?
Who put the original white paint on the new boards?
What kind of wood, where was it made?
A relic in this day of plastic and foreign-made.

They were called Cotton Region Shelters. CRS.
Developed in the southern US
Where they grow cotton.
It got hot there. Someone wanted to know how hot.

The old louvered box, with hinged door,
Almost big enough to crawl into.
Not for me, but maybe an inquisitive boy.
Also for wasps. Careful when you open the door.

Long before, it was taken by horse drawn wagon,
And placed in a clearing next to the old Ranger Station.
The old trail too rough for those new Model T's.
Taming the wilderness meant knowing its secrets.

Until recently it sat on the edge of a wildflower meadow.
Surrounded by huge spruce, flutter leafed aspen nearby.
Near the old ranger cabin in decay, logs weathered grey,
Windows frosted from years of hail and snow.

Flagpole tilted, white paint almost all gone.
The old horse corral still visible
Among the fallen and rotted aspen poles.
The old weather box tilting on its wobbly supports.

No Rangers stayed here since old Tom Willoughby
Back in '29. Right before the Depression.
He rode with Gifford and the original rangers
When the national forest was created.

Surveyed the forest, built the cabin.
Three days out from Montrose.
Around the campfire, he told stories of Griz
The wildness now a memory.

Old Weather Bureau put up the fancy white box
With the new alcohol and mercury thermometer.
Read the weather when you can. Daily hi's and lo's.
Rain, too. Would like snow, but hard to get to in the winter.

Tom complained a little,
But he read the data when he stayed there.
Hummingbird built a nest in a corner one year.
Must have tangled with the hornet nest in the other corner.

Tom forgot his pad of paper a few times.
Numbers scratched all along the bottom of the box, inside.
Were they temperatures, or maybe count on sheep
    or cattle?
One hundred forty two seems a bit high for temps here.

Will never know.
Tom left this earth back in thirty nine.
He left an old pair of spurs hanging on the back wall.
Rusted now by years of that rain he never got to measure.

Weather Bureau lost all track of the box.
Records of highs and lows disappeared
In the pile of numbers lying in yellowed file folders.
Electronic sensor down the road reads the weather now.

Sends it to a satellite, then to a computer.
Would all be foreign to Tom. He would laugh at it all.
"No one sets foot on the ground," he would say,
Then he would spit and walk away shaking his head.

He could forecast the weather by looking at the sky,
Feeling the breeze, rubbing his knees.
"You know this country or else
Get caught in a blizzard or lightning storm," he would say.

The weather box now has a new life in my yard.
Fresh coat of paint, new electronic thermometer.
It watches a different mountain now, gets less rain.
Much less snow, but much more heat.

I think of the stories it could tell.
The blizzard of '39 when it was covered by snow until June.
It stood five feet above the ground.
The lightning strike that killed the horse in the corral.

The last grizzly that wandered by, lonely,
Looking for a mate he would never find.
Wolves carefully circling the porcupine,
Huddled under the box, quills poised.

The thermometer, covered by an old hornets nest,
Stolen by some kid on a motorcycle, then tossed aside.
No bullet holes in the box. Not so the old cabin.
A modern weather man on vacation happened to see it.

Reverently, he took it down.
He understood history. A valuable find.
He cleaned it off, paint flaking, slat falling out.
Still forgotten, it went into the corner of a shed.

Similar stories, different lives.
CRS. Cotton Region Shelters.
Long way from home. Let's rename them.
ARS. Alpine region shelters.

They were part of these mountains,
Telling us part of its history, its toughness.
Life up there isn't easy. On trees, on horses.
On old Rangers who sat around a campfire.

Shadows of flames flickered on a freshly painted
Ghostly box sitting on stilts, thermometer inside.
On duty 24/7. Ready to serve.
Like old Tom the Ranger. Like Blaze, his horse.

Show a little respect as you open that door,
Hinged on the bottom. Old metal plaque
Proclaiming Property of US Weather Bureau.
Where people, not computers, once read our history.

Life goes on, like the weather,
Clouds drift by, shading the sun.
Temperatures go up, go down.
Life, like weather is a circle; no start or end, just change.

ENVIRONMENTS

The mountains: I become part of it…The herbs, the fir tree, I become part of it. The morning mists, the clouds, the gathering waters, I become part of it. The wilderness, the dew drops, the pollen…I become part of it.

~ Navajo Chant ~

GLENWOOD CANYON

I always liked the down home, simple stories told by Charles Kuralt. He somehow captured a hidden elegance and strength of human character found in ordinary everyday lives. I assumed he had some special skill in tracking down these stories.

He did have a special skill, but the stories were right in front of him. Most people are too preoccupied to see them, so we rely on someone like him to point them out to us. One brief afternoon off Interstate 70 in Glenwood Canyon, tucked in the middle of the Colorado Rockies, convinced me to start watching for any job announcement where someone would pay me to travel around catching these snippets of Americana and the goodness of humankind.

It was a sunny precursor to another springtime in the Rockies. Mid-March was a little early for that springtime; we had yet to get past the blanket of snow and month or two of additional snow yet to come. But it was warm, robins were making their way up the river valleys and the willows were swelling with their unique red and yellow luminescence. Those tantalizing days were teasers. Spring was not yet here, but we knew what to soon expect.

My wife and I were headed east, across a mountain or two and miles of grassland sea. Back across the Missouri

and Mississippi, no longer water barriers or water carriers
to the movement of a people, but now an integral part
of a civilized nation. The start of a journey always holds
promise, the end holds memories. Promises usually
end up as memories. The in-between hide success or
disappointment, but they all became a memory.

This day held many memories in the making on this
almost spring day. The place was special. Of the thousands
of miles of Interstate Highway system, I have been on
relatively few. Many of these miles cross the unending
expanse of prairie, boring to the interstate traveler
speeding I-80 across Nebraska, I-70 across Kansas, or
I-90 across the interminable reach of Montana and South
Dakota. But I doubt if there is any stretch of the Interstate
system that matches the beauty and the engineering
blend of Glenwood Canyon. The Rest Areas in this canyon
make a person feel differently than the traveler stopping
somewhere west of Russell, Kansas. The towering cliffs,
the foaming whitewater, the elevated roadway of this most
expensive of highways—all meld into an exuberance that
bursts forth from a tired traveler.

We had stopped here to eat our picnic lunch. Just
starting to examine my sandwich, I was asked by a fellow
traveler, approaching with his partner in tow, to take their
picture. "Of course," I replied. Their enjoyment of each
other was a complement to this day. With my leashed dog
Varda in tow, I waited for them to pose, then snapped a
picture. Of course Varda jerked my arm just as I snapped
the picture. They laughed. I snapped again. A memory.
They were newly married and were driving a U-Haul
from Chicago to Los Angeles. She was a traveling nurse
from Chicago; he was from LA. They had driven her car
through last week's blizzard and were now making the trip
again with the rental truck and probably all her worldly

possessions. Such is the stuff of memories to be retold
for years to come. As they drove off, heading west to
Glenwood Springs, the expanse of Utah, Vegas and their
California dream, I thought back to similar moves of my
own. Wyoming blizzards started to merge into Nebraska
blizzards, U-Hauls into moving vans, California dreams to
Utah and Colorado. What will the years do to the details of
this one chance encounter? They will thumb through their
photo album of the honeymoon years from now. Who took
this portrait of them with a rock cliff behind and blue sky
above? Oh yes, somewhere in Colorado along a river, and
some guy with a cute white dog. This picture is blurred
because the dog jumped when he took the picture. Who
was the stranger and where was he going in search of his
own past and memories fading away?

Less than five minutes later, as I was finishing my
sandwich, a young man came up to me and asked if I
could take his picture. He was with two other guys who
got out of a car with Vermont plates. College students on
spring break, of course. They were obviously in awe of
the river and this marvelous day. They posed, I snapped
and we went on our ways. My thoughts drifted back to
my memories and a similar setting. I, too, headed towards
Colorado one distant spring break. I pumped up my yellow
rubber raft on a cold Wyoming morning and dodged
moose on a river in the shadow of the Tetons. I remember
that vividly: I had river rafting permit number 1 for 1968
for the Snake River. I look now at my own snapshots and
think of the promise, the successes and the failures. All
memories. Enjoy it now, guys from Vermont. It will never
be as carefree and fun as now.

Finishing my lunch, I saw another young couple park
their truck with Arizona plates next to ours. I saw the
camera in his hand. Taking him by surprise, I quickly

asked "would you like me to take your picture? That seems
to be my reason for being here today." He hesitated, then
said OK. I think he was a little uncertain but they realized
the value of a picture at this point in their lives.

I waited as they posed. He said "one, two, three."
On three, he lifted her in the air as I snapped. They
were obviously oblivious to the world and enjoying only
each other. I asked if they were married. He almost
shouted in glee that she had just said "Yes!" This indeed
was a memory worth capturing on film. He made it
even more memorable to me as he continued. She was
from South Africa; they met in Disneyland and were
now traveling somewhere in blissful glee, just having
agreed to pursue their memories together. Today was
their beginning of forever. He asked about my wife and
me. I said, "We are going on 28 years together." I think
he was awed by that. I thought back. Yes, it was rather
surprising. Twenty-eight years ago, we shared similar
expectations. Our lives had first come together in the
wonderland of Mt. Rainier National Park, then joined
into one on the rim of the Grand Canyon. From there, we
found our home moving from Colorado to Michigan to
California to Utah to South Dakota, finally to Colorado
again. I could have spent hours giving advice and
suggestions. I instead said, "Have fun." That's probably
the most useful suggestion I could give. The years go by,
the rivers flow March through November. People and
friends come and go. Dreams glow and fade. We always
seem to be on a journey somewhere. Some memories
start, some end, many continue always changing.

We watched the two walk hand-in-hand down the path
as we slowly packed up the remnants of lunch. I looked for
more people to take pictures of. None came. It was time to
move on. Three encounters, three different stories. Mine

made a fourth. Life was full of promise on this eventful day. Friday the 13th. How many more stories were passing by on this busy highway? Mine was headed east, in search of the spirit of Charles Kuralt, myself, and the lives that become memories for us all.

The Smoke of Summer

The smothering blanket of smoke from distant wildfires had become a familiar sight to me. Every year, at some point during the summer, I found myself flying from Grand Junction to Salt Lake City en route to my newest assignment as Public Information Officer for wildfires. June of 2008 found me flying towards my latest assignment via Phoenix. Looking out the plane window, down through the layers of smoke, the usually brown landscape lay blurred far below. If I were down there in the blanket of smoke, I would be choked by the haze, but the smell of the remnants of tree and brush would take me to distant memories of flame and excitement. Those memories detailed younger days, digging fire line, hiking to remote hillsides guided by the smell of burning trees.

The announcement from the captain that we were descending into Sacramento gave truth to the subtle shift I noticed in the plane as we circled down, slower, steeper. Looking out the window told me nothing. In our smothering cloud of smoke, we saw no movement until the runway reached up to grab our wheels. The great Sacramento Valley of California, the land of sunshine, was hidden in the smoke of countless fires. When I finally stepped out of the confines of the airport terminal, I breathed deeply. A gentle smell of wood smoke from a forest far enough away to have tempered the bite said hello. But it was still a forest fire. I smiled at the memories it raised.

I drove north on I-5, through unfamiliar territory even

in sunshine, which was unseen above the smoke this June morning. I was tired from flying and an unscheduled overnight stay in Phoenix, sans luggage due to a missed connecting flight. Due, by the way, to smoke closing Sky Harbor and delaying the flight from Junction. I was still without luggage and on my way to the unknown future that envelops all fire assignments. My destination: Willows and the Mendocino National Forest, nestled on the west side of the Great Valley and hidden, along with all of northern California, in this vast blanket of smoke.

As in a dream, I put the car in cruise control and watched the blurry fields pass by. Sunflowers sat in full bloom, all bright yellow heads pointing east, searching for the hidden sun. The plants were small, not even two feet tall, topped by the seed we humans compete for with countless bird feeders. Slightly droopy, soon to be stiffened, unable to swing like a yellow metronome, the seeds were bursting with oily nutrition. They reminded me of cheerful dwarves, marching off to adventure, captured in a snapshot of frozen motion. The haze added mystery to this happy scene, more used to the blinding brilliance of Valley sunshine.

The yellow fields merged into almond orchards, dull in comparison. Loaded with ripening nuts, the limbs hung like dejected basset ears. Plowed ground underneath, the stands seemed bare and sparse, months having passed since their flowering glory under foggy February skies. Other fields of something unknown to me appeared between the main crops. They looked like weeds, but I knew the value of this rich farmland would not allow a square inch to go to anything as wasteful as a weed. A little used railroad paralleled the freeway, with a falling down old telephone line tagging along like a lost pup. Wires dangled, poles leaned, voices hadn't streamed along these wires for decades. The line whispered to me of an era long turned to dust. The smoke took me back further, centuries further.

My thoughts faded beyond the fields, the orchards, the railroad. They wandered past the gold seekers racing to the mountains which lined the valley to the east. They settled on a valley flooded by a shallow sea of fresh water during the rain of foggy winters and the snow melt of the Sierra spring time, soon to be quickly dried by the searing sun of a cloudless July.

A smoke-filled sky from burning forests of centuries past hid the glacial tops of the shining Sierra. Grizzlies wandered the vast plains, exploring the meandering miles-wide streams choked with flailing salmon. Bands of nearly naked people huddled over hollowed rocks, pounding acorns. They were used to the smoke. They casually moved out of the way, looking forward to the new life inhabiting the burned-off brush fields. The smoke hid nothing but the view of far off hills. The promise of this unrivaled fertile soil and a climate perfect for growing food all lay in the future.

As I ignored the smoke-blurred view of reality, I thought of what the smoke would have hidden in this far-off time of my imagination. Pioneers of any land see only the future. They ignore the treasure they inevitably destroy. Is there no compromise? Is there no way to go back, to tell them they are destroying one to create another? The dream of something better is too subjective. "Better" is never understood. The grizzly doesn't know the meaning of the word. Is the sun better than the fog? Not to the fog itself. Is clear air better than the smoke that chokes the breath? Not to the soil that absorbs the life-giving nutrients of the smoke.

The word "better" doesn't exist to the geese, the

mountains, and the flames themselves. The goose sees only the smoke and it fills the air as far as the goose can fly. The mountains see only the thunderstorms and blizzards. Our lifetime is only a blink to the rock and streams. The flames see only the breeze that carries them to renewed life.

The opaqueness of this smothering smoke causes the mind to travel back to times that live no longer on this Earth. The sun must explode and another regroup from the dust before a valley can flood again and fill with salmon and grizzlies hidden among waving fields of grass and flowers.

The pioneers and miners who flooded the valley with humanity, replacing the natural flood of rain and meltwater, destroyed my chance to enjoy what they saw. They looked at the scene but didn't really see it. They saw a different potential and riches. They then quickly proceeded to destroy the potential and riches for me.

In the meantime, I had to be satisfied with seeing the sunflowers shining through the haze. So I smiled at the yellow rows. They were the best I had left to enjoy. They looked brighter already as I contemplated the future.

FLIGHT OF THE CATTAIL DOWN

The late November afternoon sun dimmed its brilliance, playing hide and seek with a high, thin haze of clouds. But still its rays were enough to warm me as I sat on the open hillside, not blinded by its glare as I was earlier in the day. The dog and I settled onto the ground, nesting in a hollow in the rocky dirt to meditate on the scene. Actually, Goldberry was meditating on the smells, in her own flow of energy, while I tried to connect Earth's energy with my own deficient senses.

Before I could concentrate on trying to see the energy of the trees and rocks, I was distracted by thousands if not millions of floating bursts of energy. I was on a hillside above a cattail-covered stream bottom, mottled by dappled sunlight shaded by the ridge high above. The cattail seeds danced a hypnotizing ballet, a three dimensional artwork. The air was an explosion of white, back-lit by the sinking sun. Some miniature parachutes rose lazily like hot air balloons seeking the heavens. Some drifted back down. A few shot downward like meteors. Others wafted by the slightest breeze headed upstream; the undecided circled around trying to choose where they were headed. There was very little wind, but the invisible lift of heated air rising off the rocks and hillside carried the white fuzz upward, shooting off the prehistoric spikes of the cattail forest.

The only comparison I could make was to a gentle snowfall, but even with a swirling wind, snowflakes do not rise upwards dozens of feet. It was a sculpture in motion.

I tried to follow the delicate parachutes as they lifted off. Some rose above me, others drifted out of sight to the north, powered by the gentle waft of a gossamer breath of breeze. I envisioned the circling descent of sandhill cranes, another prehistoric image, as they settled to earth after a long flight. The bare twigs and branches of dead junipers surrounding me were covered with the same white fuzz, like the down on a young crane. The luminescent coat covered everything in the vicinity. Seeds never to germinate, but that was alright since only one in a million was needed to replenish the cattail stand, and there were thousands being shot into the sky with each breath of air.

I focused on the cattail spikes. I felt sorry for anyone who has never stood among November cattails on a warm, sunny afternoon and squeezed the flower spike. The first time I did it, I made the mistake of standing down breeze, quickly enveloped in a cloud of puffy seed. The slow motion explosion of fuzzy featherdown bursts into the sky like a New Year's Eve celebration. It is the celebration of the cattail to end one life and begin another. It has gone on for millions of years.

Goldberry sneezed as a drifting seed hit her nose. An occasional breeze realigned the fluffs of white into a determined flight upstream. Then, when the breeze stopped, the parachutes resumed their drift upwards, downwards, sideways. The time release capsule of seed puffs alternated from cattail to cattail. They were sufficient to last for days. Some were just beginning to swell up, others were half eaten away. The standing forest of long, slender cattail leaves shone brilliantly in the autumn light. The nearby grasses stood regally upright, awaiting the first snow to lay them horizontal.

I memorized this scene before I stood up to leave. It was the last tribute to autumn before life settled under a white blanket of snow, matting the seeds until a dry winter thaw sent the remaining parachutes on a last sail. The sun dropped below the hilltop to the west. Night was coming. I failed to see the energy aura surrounding the trees on this meditative excursion, but I lived inside an atom of energy for a few moments. It was a worthy trade.

Aspen Gold

The conditions were perfect, taking me back over 40 years. It was a late September afternoon, the sky a blinding clear blue dotted with a few small cumulus clouds, their white highlighting the edges of blue. This year, there was an abundance of reddish color to the usual golden yellow aspen leaves dotting the towering white trunks. The aspen clones edged the deep blue-green of the spruce forest and the tan grass of the spent summer meadows. Few wildflowers had survived this far into the autumn of this high country.

I sat reveling in the sacredness of the setting. It was coming home to a place I had sadly missed much of the past few years. Life had gotten in the way of a ritual of living in the moment of the aspen autumn.

I thought back 44 years to when I came home for the first time to my cathedral of the mountains. It was along the Conejos River in southern Colorado. I had a new life: a new wife, a new home, a new job, a new dog. I was living a dream come true. As a boy awaiting the moment to leave the flat boring farm lands of central Illinois, I had worshipped the far off Rocky Mountains. Now I was there. That summer was an experience learning a different life, but the autumn was a serendipity. The aspen stands in this part of my dreamed Colorado were more than a fantasy come true. There were pure stands of nothing but white and yellow. There were also pure stands of stately spruce. There were other stands of aspen with a young spruce understory slowly edging out the aspen. All this was mixed with the meadows and grasslands of tan and brown. Spent wildflowers still dotted the meadows, washed by time of the faded glory of their reds, yellows and blues of summer.

The hummingbirds had by now fled south; the silent elk prowled the forests, ready to call forth in the upcoming rut. But mostly, the quiet was overpowering. A light breeze would ruffle the yellow leaves, releasing some leaves to twirl slowly to a growing yellow mat of forest carpet. For the first time of many times to come, I expressed my personal phrase of autumn: the falling leaves would "whirl, twirl and swirl" in a shower of yellow floating to the ground in slow motion.

But on this day in the year 2014, long distanced from that first fall of 1970, memories replaced the real view before me. I thought of the years along the southern Colorado rivers Conejos and Rio Grande, then in the forests bordering North Park in the headwaters of the North Platte in northern Colorado. After a brief interlude in the foothills of California along the east side of the Sierra Nevada northwest of Reno, I rediscovered the massive aspen stands of the Rocky Mountains, this time in southern Utah on the sides of Boulder Mountain.

Now, in retirement, I called the forests of western Colorado home. Colorado once again. Other mountains of the West have aspen, but nothing compares to those in Colorado. And nothing can compare with the late days of September, under the autumn bluebird skies capping the hillsides of gold and white. It was usually a short-lived display. Already on this day, I noticed with a tinge of sadness that some stands were past their prime. The color was nearly gone, the stark naked white of the trunks standing sentinel until next spring.

I thought myself to be like the stands of autumn aspen. The glory of springtime had come and gone in a whirlwind of adventure. The maturing of summer had brought new memories, but the hiking and exploring was slowing down. Now, the colorful burst of autumn foretold of a winter of endings. Winter was still a distant view, but I could now see it approaching.

I always found autumn the most interesting time of year, with the shutting down of the fast pace of spring and summer. Life was created, it grew, blossomed, and sped past in a flurry of activity. But now it was ready to slow down, to savor the life lived and get ready for a long rest.

The aspen were doing that. Their leaves quivered in the breeze; they flew the flag of maturity and wisdom, and when the time was ready, they lay down to sleep, preparing the world for a new burst of life in a few more months. I liked the part about wisdom. I thought of my life and the lives of those with whom I had shared time. We had matured to a point where we now had wisdom. Some had gone on without me. My beloved four-leggeds had shared many adventures of exploration. Strider, Gandalf, and Varda had gone on ahead, past the winter of their lives. Goldberry was in her time of winter, slowing down as was I. Was I facing my winter as well?

I looked into the forest roof, the spires of spruce green, the yellow of aspen perched on top of white trunks. All of this reaching into the brilliant blue of that autumn sky. Modern life was too fast, too shortsighted, too greedy. Sometimes I found it hard to slow down. Patience was not a virtue for me. But how can one sit or lie down in a golden yellow aspen grove on a day like this and not get lost in a time warp? Life slowed to a crawl, to a pace like the never ending floating of a golden leaf to the ground below the white trunked sentinel. The blue of the sky held the leaves like a magnet, begging them to float upwards to form yellow clouds that would rain golden drops of nectar.

I looked upwards to the sky, then down to cloud, then

to tree top and finally to falling leaves. My eyes followed the brown trunks of stately spruce downward. They caressed the white of the aspen trunks down to the golden carpet. A woodpecker flittered from one tree to the next. The raven scolded me as he flew from one meadow to the next. I waited for a bugle of the elk, but it was too early for him to search for his mate. Maybe in a week or two. But by then, a light snowfall might blanket the earth like a mother covering her young with a blanket of warmth.

It was ever-changing and I had to grab a new memory before it left in its never ending cycle of life. That's what made it bearable for me. I would miss the afternoon warmth of a sun shining down from a blue sky onto a green and white and golden world below. I would marvel at the soon-to-be coating of white on all life below, but the sky would remain blue and my memories would remain sacred. I got up to leave, silently saying goodbye once again for another year. The swirl of golden leaves nodded to me on their fall to earth. I think they would miss my admiration of them, but they wouldn't dwell on it. They were planning already for next year, after a long and peaceful sleep.

INTERLUDE:
ASPEN IN THE ROCKS OF HEAVEN

Feet in the earth,
Arms in the sky.
Planted in rock,
Seeming to fly.

They stand as guardians
Of a rocky home.
They search for wisdom
In the boundless unknown.

Nearby trees are taller,
Painting hillsides green.
Other aspen straighter,
Reaching for clouds unseen.

The autumn yellow gone
As leaves blanket their feet.
Grass is now golden.
Winds whisper of snow and sleet.

Their forms are dancers,
Twirling in joyous glee.
Their hopes are reaching,
As far as eyes can see.

They stand atop the world,
Most life exists below.
They seek to find and learn
All we cannot know.

Their forms are ghosts
Whispering a magic tale.
Their lives spent in search
Of their own holy grail.

They know, we don't
Answers we cannot learn.
Life is free and joyous
At every twist and turn.

They bend and twirl,
Branches now hard and dead.
White has left the bark
It turns to gray instead.

Sentinels of the mesa top
Guarding their rocky crest.
They curl and curve, then stop,
And laugh at all the rest.

They have the answers we need
As we learn their hidden worth.
We ask, their answer a creed:
Seek for heaven, keep your feet on earth.

They dance with outstretched arms
And laugh as the winds blow by.
Their view is eternity
We can only ask why.

Their leaves have left
As winds clean the air.
Blown to hidden clefts
Strewn from here to there.

Treasures of golden hair.
Have floated in the breeze
Lacy arms now white and bare
Blanketing meadows with leaves.

Their leaves have fallen
Trunks twirl and twist
Bare arms now sullen
They fade into the mist.

INTERLUDE:
MT. RAINIER FANTASY

The mountain looms, majestic, overpowering.
It rules the sky, the land, the distant bay.
It spoke loudly, many times.
It will speak again, we fear.

Born of fire, bathed in ice
Its feet in green and a kaleidoscope of colors
It creates life, then destroys it.
It toys with us, unsure of what to do.

We tiptoe around her feet
Admiring the beauty, ignoring the power.
The power is hidden, by religious awe.
The beauty is on display, we will worship that.

I left the carpet of forest down below,
Trudged up the snow, then the ice.
Blinding bright, even in the early morning pink
    that precedes the sun.
Rock crags protruding like ships at sea.

The summit looks close enough to touch.
It is miles away, towering in the cloud.
Distance is deceiving. I walk and walk,
Getting no closer.

The pack gains weight,
Defying laws of physics.
Legs tire, breath comes harder.
I never meant to reach the summit; just testing the ice.

I retreat to the forest below.
It is a safe haven for me, the deer, the buttercups.
And the berries. Hillsides of berries.
Huckleberry, salmonberry, strawberry, thimbleberry.

My mouth waters at the thought.
The mountain waters are the reality.
Streams, crystal clear and pure,
Cascade and tumble through flower-filled meadows.

Bouncing off rocks, mist bathing
    the monkey flowers at stream's edge.
Clear pools, then foaming falls,
Ice cold, it numbs my bare toes,
Wiggling in the spray of the white fury of foam.

Follow the stream down where it joins the river.
Meandering among the giants.
Ancient cedars, red strips of bark, trunk disappearing
    in the moss,
Hiding in the bunchberry dogwood and ferns.

It is cool down here, the smell so fresh,
    it bathes my very soul.
Sunlight fights to reach the ground,
Shattered into rays that come from heaven.
You can almost see the angels singing their praise.

The river leaves the meadow and jumps downhill,
Silver Falls takes a plunge over an edge of basalt.
Stand underneath and watch the drops
     flatten and come apart.
Rainbows dance across the moss, spray turns to mist,
     drifting in all directions.

The river turns to thunder, a white torrent
Bouncing off rocks immersed in the flood.
You feel the power, the awe.
Melting snow only hours before.

The water has changed in its frenzy of downward fall.
It's going home, to the far away sea,
To meet the whales, the salmon, the crying gulls.
It rests there before renewing its never ending cycle.

I leave the river, wander back to the ridge.
The eyes relax in the textured weaving of green.
It undulates in pointed spires, over ridge
     and down the valley.
Eventually joining the fields of snow and ice
     back where we began.

It is a painting, a symphony, sweet and mouthwatering.
I lose myself in transcendent meditation.
It is power yet it is a fragile lacework
As delicate as the swallowtail floating by on the breeze.

Stare at the mountain long enough
And you will never be the same.
It envelops you and pulls you into itself.
You have witnessed a preview of heaven.

BREEZES

*While we are born with curiosity and wonder
and our early years full of the adventure they bring,
I know such inherent joys are often lost.
I also know that, being deep within us, their latent glow
can be fanned to flame again by awareness
and an open mind.*

Sigurd Olson, *Listening Point*

SILENCE

Is there a silence more profound than that of a snowfall in a calm nighttime forest? I pondered that as I walked out my door into new fallen snow on a frozen January morning. Yes, there are several situations that rival it, I thought. The quiet of a foggy March morning in a California redwood forest. Or the whisper of a May breeze across the grassy expanse of South Dakota prairie.

I enjoy the quiet of nature, but sometimes I wonder if I belong to a dying breed. A breed that shake their heads in confusion at the preponderance of cell phones, pagers, dinging laptops and other assorted and noisy gadgetry of modern society. Are people afraid of silence? Do they fear to hear their own thoughts or the blood coursing through their veins?

I like to sit on a lichen-covered rock and stare off at the distant mountains. I am enthralled at the symphony of silence available to me any time of day on any day of the year. I love the quiet, but even more I love the gentlest interruptions. A chickadee tells me I should be refilling the feeder by the front deck. A titmouse comes to see if I have peanuts for him. I haven't taken the time to train him to eat out of my hand like his grandparents did. I know a few words of titmouse and chickadees (they speak the same language): "feed me."

My meditation is occasionally broken by the roar of a golden eagle as he races past me at treetop level, the wind exploding past his feathered arms. The first time I heard it, I thought it was a jet fighter gone astray. I think he does it on purpose, knowing its shock value to me. Why else would he interrupt his endless circling as a speck high up in the heavens to come down and raise the hackles on my neck? I thought I heard him laughing the last time he flew by.

The breeze always creates a symphony worthy of Mozart. The juniper needles rustle softly, but the grass is even softer. If I listen hard enough, I hear the individual blades of grass dancing to the rhythm of the wind, fresh off the distant Utah desert.

As the quiet deepens, I sway to the tinkle and burble of the creek below. It is steady and unending, yet ever changing and never boring. It is the ultimate lullaby. A slight shift in the wind brings the melody to a high pitch, which then fades back to a whisper.

But the best sounds of silence are in the dark of night. A crack of a twig from some unknown prowler. A hoot from the far off owl or the yip of a passing coyote over on the next ridge. Night sounds are always far off, yet the dark brings them right underfoot. If I give them time, they turn into friendly voices. But that I rarely do. Time seems to be turning into something as rare nowadays as silence. I try, but I am too impatient.

That is when I need to sit down and let the silence bring me more time. Most people may not realize this quiet little fact. Silence creates time. I can sit listening to the quiet of the breeze, the patience of the centuries-old gnarled juniper trees, the wisdom of the lichen painted on the basalt rocks. And when I let go of the trance I am in, I come back to real time. I discover I was only sitting there a few minutes. My mind traveled eons back in time and I savored the stories the silence told me.

It is magic. But when I leave my home up here on the mesa with the chickadees and eagles to travel down into town, I enter a different universe. I am shocked into reality by the traffic on the highway, the blaring stereo in the pickup next to me, the continuous chattering of people walking down the street talking into cell phones. What is so important to these people? Can't they walk, or shop, or drive in silence?

I do my errands, then hurry back to my quiet retreat. The silence has become a close friend. I wait for the next snowy night so I can bundle up for the cold, go outside and listen to each snowflake fall and twirl to earth. Each one carries a message to me. It says "listen."

I Know There Is a God

I know there is a God when I hear a full symphony backing Luciano Pavarotti send the reverberations of "Nessun Dorma" across the canyons and cliffs of the Colorado River entrenched into the Utah canyons. The endless expanse of time exposed in the reds and oranges of the sandstones laid in deserts and oceans of an earth that knew not dinosaurs yet. The power of a windstorm and a raindrop, expanded by 1000 million sunsets, convinces me God is a poet and sculptor telling a story we have yet to interpret.

I know there is a god when I listen to Andrea Bocelli sing the beautifully haunting "Sogno." I lay on the ground looking up at a sky framed by glowing green needles of towering yellow barked pines. The late afternoon sun lights the bottlebrush branches into a green that highlights the blue of the Colorado sky, a blue so brilliant, so pure, it brings tears to my eyes. A blue that was what God intended when she decided on a color of a sky that hid the heaven beyond. A small white cloud drifts overhead with a white so bright, it is a sun unto itself. I was once asked what my favorite color was. I replied it is the bluebird blue of a Colorado sky where it meets the pure puffy white of a passing cloud. Yes, it can convince you that God does exist.

I know there is a God when I hear John Denver sing "Rocky Mountain High." As I sit high in a mountain valley as a July thunderstorm passes by, listening to the thunder bounce echoes off rocky peaks towering above a small snow-fringed lake, I know there is also a heaven. I know because I am in it. Heaven is the hummingbird flittering over the flower beds of gentian and harebell, buttercup and forget-me-not. It is the crisp freshness of the meadow that stretches up to the tundra, where you can see past the horizon and wish you could walk forever. I will someday.

We seem to have confused a god who lives in our midst and has created a heaven we cannot see or feel or hear with some religious deity who guides our lives as if we were so helpless, we could not function without divine guidance. That may be the ultimate God for some, but for me, I will take my God now, as a power that has unselfishly given me my heaven to enjoy in this life.

How can I not acknowledge that power when I watch the eagle soar over the valley, lifting on thermals I cannot see, seeing details I didn't know existed? Or when I watch the pika flit from rock to rock, high above a timberline that erects a stop sign to the upward flow of the magnificent spruce and aspen that line the mountain slopes below with a green carpet. Or when I huddle from a January blizzard that lays a white blanket to protect that heaven in a silent sleep while the sun hovers on the southern horizon. Are we so blind and deaf that we are missing these treasures we have been given? Too many of us sit and wait for miracles to guide us. These miracles are before us now.

As I sit here in a pine-fringed meadow, I watch a deer poke its way along the flowered carpet. The breeze flitters the aspen leaves, moves across the grass like an ocean wave. I let the voice of John Denver overpower the chickadee scolding me from its hidden perch. Denver has taken me back in time to the magic of earlier days, when he and I were discovering the magic of the mountains. The bluest sky I ever imagined when my life was beginning anew and I was trading in that God of the religions to the God I was living with.

Yes, I know there is a God when I sit by a mountain

stream, ice cold with nearby snowmelt, and hear the strains of "Amazing Grace" sung a cappella by Joan Baez. The haunting melody, coming from the very clouds above, drifts with the water as it gurgles and burbles over rocks and moss, guarded by red and yellow monkey flowers and white puffs of cottongrass, disappearing into the echoing depths of willows. It is the definition of peace and hope.

I know there is a God as I stand on the lakeshore, watching the small waves lap the grassy shore, listening to Peter, Paul, and Mary paint the waves with the sorrow and loss of "Where Have All the Flowers Gone." An anthem of my youth, a cry of sanity in insane times; I regain that sanity now, my purpose in a time of despair. I do wonder where all the flowers have gone, gone from a time so long ago when we were young and changing the world. The lake will change as well, but on a time scale lost to me. The sky blue lake will turn into a grassy flower studded meadow where one day a doe will meander along, nibbling the flowers.

There are so many signs, so much peace and beauty, so much hope, if we can only see and hear and feel. There are so many works of man that can add to this heavenly setting. There is so much time, if only we allow it to happen.

I come up into the high country to relax and refresh. I forget I was coming home to a promise I first met years ago. I want to share it with everyone. There is room for each of us to sit in our own meadow, saying our own prayer. I will be quiet now and reacquaint myself with my God. I just pray we don't destroy it all before I finish.

A WILDERNESS OF THE SOUL

The call for official Wilderness designation has calmed down in recent years, although passions about this legal and symbolic sanctification still exist. The large battles of thirty and forty years ago, though, have faded into the memories of battle scarred veterans like me. I used to think we needed to designate many acres of wilderness, a tangible sign of our environmental victories over the short sighted wastefulness of a growing civilization. We were awakening as a people and civilized society to the need to protect our very existence as a part of Mother Nature. Wilderness was one way to shout 'stop' to our destructive nature. But it missed a key part of the equation. Saving acres of rock and ice, desert and canyon did mean something, but more important was the basic land ethic so many were ignorant of. We missed this as we focused on the big legislative victories.

I stand on the edge of the canyon now and look into a wilderness that prohibits many things. It even encourages some behavior. Those who venture into it bow down, enjoy the silence, bask in the primitive nature of the place. Others watch from the edges, grousing about their exclusion as they rev the engines of their four wheelers. Then they all leave, reentering the non-wilderness world they are still ravaging. Some still clamor for the big W for the red rock expanse of southern Utah, one of the few remaining roadless expanses in the interior West. Their voices lack the passion of decades ago. I smile at the sincerity still evident, but I know these are the outliers of the battle, the skirmishes of those who came too late for the real battles. Those times are gone. We fought. We won some, we lost many more. But we lost the larger war. We now have islands surrounded by the smoking ruins of everything else. The grizzly still hang on, a few more wolves roam the forests, the peregrines fly with more company, but the larger picture is a sad remnant of a glory in its decline.

We may have gained a presidential signature on a piece of paper, a gray routed sign, a colored line on a map. We lost the message to everyone that told of our myopia. We bred ourselves into a desperate need to drown ourselves, like lemmings flying over a cliff. We lost that basic land ethic that Aldo Leopold, John Muir, Bob Marshall, and scores of others preached to an obviously empty forest of bodies, intent on racing forward at full speed. We lost the heart and soul of the young who will never know true wilderness, that sense of awe and belonging to a larger unknown. What have we gained in the intervening decades since I and the shock troops of the environmental movement charged full speed at increasing acres of Wilderness?

I have gained a pessimism, a melancholy memory, a sadness of a lost civilization. Some call it the end of nature. I say no to that. Nature will continue on quite well, thank you. Our part in it? Well, that may be the more important question. Nature is amoral. Nature has cast off nearly every single species since the first amoeba squirmed out of the ooze. Of course I cry for the disappearance of wolves, polar bears, even the timid pikas living in the warming mountain tops of rock. But more importantly I cry for my descendants, who may never know the freedom I have seen vanish. But then, even I have seen only a shadow of the vast panorama of wild nature that my ancestors only a few dozen generations removed were able to see. We may lay claim to a smudge on a map. We may have lost claim to everything else.

It is easy to be pessimistic. It is harder to put that aside and struggle to regain some optimism. The more we lose, the harder it is to regain it. Some is beyond redemption. That is truly the pessimistic part. I can stand along the Lolo Divide and guess what Lewis and Clark experienced. I can disappear onto the endless horizon of big and little bluestem on a few remnant acres of prairie and sense what the earliest French courier de bois or Spanish conquistadors found threatening and uneasy to them. But I have not known and cannot know that true feeling.

There was no such thing as wilderness to the aboriginal tribes that wandered here for thousands of years. They felt at home everywhere and uneasy nowhere. But they didn't leave anything that detracted from what we now consider to be wilderness. They left only traces of their being. Were they the saints some claim them to be? No, they were human just like us. Even if they had the technology and equipment to leave behind roads and buildings, dams and huge holes in the ground, would they have?

We will never know. And we will never really understand their theology and faith that seemed to guide their lives. But my guess is they would still honor what they considered sacred. Sacred is a concept that goes with wilderness. It is indeed sacred, as precious as any holy book we can now write as this so called "civilized people."

Many people have said that wilderness is a state of mind. It certainly is, and I have found wilderness right next to a lonely mountain road, looking across the valley at a clear cut, underneath a sky full of jet contrails. But it certainly is more enjoyable in the capital W wilderness areas, small as they usually are. I have never been in the genuine wilderness of Alaska, where my life could be in danger at all times. I think I would be afraid, yet I would ease into a satisfaction that I could survive, assuming I eventually did survive.

In the meantime, we grab onto what we can and dream the dreams our distant ancestors did. Life itself was a struggle with no safety assured anywhere at any time. Maybe that is what we are searching for. We have gotten too comfortable and know too well what we can expect.

I am confident at some point, we will return to a wilderness of life. Humans in their over-civilized world of technology and comfort may have evolved into something else by then, but nature cannot abandon the concept of true wilderness. A wilderness where we are welcome everywhere, as long as we observe what is and should be sacred.

SUN STANDS STILL

We call it the winter solstice, but we are prejudiced by our location in the cold and snow of northern latitudes. This is certainly not the solstice of winter in Argentina or New South Wales. They swelter in the heat of summer. So let's call it the December solstice, or the northern solstice. It still means the same.

It means the sun is falling into the southern horizon, allowing the darkness and the frost of polar realms to permeate our climate, our vision, and our souls. We become short and irritable from lack of sunlight, cabin bound as snow and frigid darkness move us inside in front of the fire. We react to age old instincts from our primitive ancestors, not understanding the celestial movements. We believed the shamans and bone rattlers as they told us to pray to the god or goddess of the sun, of warmth, of greenery. Back in the times when vast ice sheets hemmed us in, we peered over our shoulders looking for the Neanderthal stumbling down the willow bound creek. We knew a lot of fear back then. We wondered who we had angered that they would steal our sun. By then we had gotten used to it, but we still said a silent prayer urging the sun to come back to us. It happened every year, but would it without our constant urging? We have learned a lot since then, but sometimes I wonder how much.

Solstice. From the Latin meaning "sun standing still." It for sure does stand still, frozen low in the southern sky at this snowy and bone-chilling time. For almost three weeks, it hangs in about the same low spot, heatless, with long shadows. It rises far to the southeast at almost the same time each morning, and it sets at almost the same time each evening low in the southwest. We have to refine our measurements to tell when solstice is. The ancients solved the problem, and without clocks. We still marvel at their precision. Most people had little concept of time. Some shamans did. It all revolves around the earth's revolution around the sun, tilted as it is.

If we lived along the Amazon, or in Singapore, or on the plains of the Serengeti, all along the equator, we wouldn't think of such things. There, the sun stays civilized, overhead and relentless to a fault. But we didn't stay near the Serengeti and towering Kilimanjaro. We roamed in all directions, seeking something we didn't understand, which we still don't understand. We went much further north than we did south. We hit glaciers and ice and cold. And darkness. So we invented celebrations and festivals and prayers. We called one of them solstice. How many religions celebrate something at about this time?

Solstice. The sun stands still, pondering, ready to make a significant change. There is some magic to it. We hang crystals, light candles, sing incantations. We pray, we dance, we revert to the magical, the mystical. There is mystery, much more than we can understand. And celebrations certainly don't hurt. If they soothe our souls, the very DNA that has accompanied us for so many million years, well, all the better.

Let us dedicate the return of the sun to a return of sanity and hope for our future. The sun will return, we will regenerate, the soil will warm, rains will come, and flowers will bloom once again. Then, each year, at a time when the sun stands still with the heat late at night, we will gather again and say farewell to that relentless friend that decides to return south, where southern people beg it to come their way. It is a tug and pull that has gone on as long as the oceans have sent endless waves pounding on the shores. And it will continue, regardless of our efforts to wish and celebrate.

Interlude: Lazuli

The bird feeder hangs from a low branch,
Outside the kitchen window.
As I wash dishes, I watch them feeding.

The birds change, winter to summer.
Always scrambling, hanging, hopping
    from branch to feeder.
Often down onto the ground to pick up their dribbles.

All have personalities from greedy to greedier.
Except my favorite,
The delicate painting called lazuli bunting.

He arrives in the spring, along with the hummers.
He sits quietly, in blue and russet dignity.
If he has a song, I don't know it.

He doesn't scrabble, like the jays or finches.
The ground hugging juncos have left by then,
The nuthatch hops on the feeder, grabs
    a sunflower seed, then disappears.

The jay is the flying pig, throwing food around
    like it was free.
He can empty the feeder in minutes,
Carpeting the ground with seed
    that the doves huddle around.

But the lazuli sits with silent grace
That tells other birds to stay away for awhile.
The maestro is on stage. Sit there and watch
    how it should be done.

He does not dominate, he does not fight.
He picks a seed delicately, munches it, looks
    around to enjoy the scenery.
Then another and another. His aura says perfection.

His color is a painting of excellence:
    blue and russet and white.
The sky above, the earth below, white the clouds
    in between.
I can watch him all day.

If a bully does approach, he leaves.
Dignity does not scrabble, flit nor fly around.
When the scramble is over, he returns, to pick
    one seed at a time.

INTERLUDE:
THE POLLINATORS

They fly with diaphanous wings.
Flitter, and float, bouncing on air.
All shapes and sizes, ugly and beauty and grace.

They are the insects
In the air, on the ground, hopping and buzzing.
They outnumber us, humble us in their complexity.

We will ignore the unpleasantness,
The biters, suckers, irritating ones.
They exist, leave it at that.

Let us glory in the flower lovers.
They complement the color.
A mix of petals, wings, pollen and bodies.

Colors subtle and bright,
Reds and greens, blues and oranges.
No artist with palette and brush can arrange color as well.

The tiger swallowtail just flew by.
She floats and paints the sky with her wings.
No ballet dancer achieves more poise.

The damselfly, in iridescent blue
Screams by in jet powered aim.
Yet stops mid flap and hovers.

Small bees and flies,
Names unknown, numbers unseen.
The workhorses of pollination.

Flowers call to them
Come visit me, I will feed you sweet nectar.
They come, life continues, they move on, successful.

I once thought all bees were honey.
Or bumble, the heavies.
Not so, oh no, not so.

Bees fill the air around the Virginia creeper.
Their buzzing cacophony is itself a symphony.
But look closely.

Filter out the noise and see the bees.
They are small, then smaller still.
They are black, brown, striped, spotted.

Crawling, bouncing, darting, hovering.
There are as many kinds as I can see colors.
As I can hear buzzes.

They are joined by butterflies, damselflies.
Real flies, strange flies.
How can there be so many?

How do they find one another to mate?
Can we imagine people like that?
Are you a person or a sort of person; maybe a non person?

Don't call them bugs.
They are a universe unto themselves.
As foreign to us as we to them.

Listen to their hum, their whirr, the buzz.
Absorb their colors, their patterns
As they absorb pollen.

Life comes in many shapes
Many forms, many patterns.
Can we feel its beauty?

I would love to hover over a flower filled vine
And drink in wisdom as they drink nectar.
Could I ever learn enough to fill my cup?

THE STORIES BEHIND
THE STORIES

*Only the mountain has lived long enough
to listen objectively to the howl of a wolf.*

Aldo Leopold, *Sand County Almanac*

BEHIND THE STORIES

Sometimes the story that created the essay or poem was as interesting as the writing itself. It certainly lends some context. I share these events that resulted in the essays and poems.

On the Rim. We started exploring the Moab country after I retired and settled in the North Fork Valley. Our new home was less than 100 miles (as the raven flies) east across the Uncompahgre Plateau from that expanse of red rock. We discovered the Utah slickrock country in the late 80's when I was working on the Dixie National Forest, adjacent to Capitol Reef National Park. I fell in love with the geology and the canyons of this magical land. When we first drove out to the Canyon Rim overlook south of Moab, we were taken literally breathless at the view. Hiking along the rim gives one the wonder and magnificence of the view of the Colorado River and the Maze across the way, but also at the simple and delicate beauty of the trees, flowers, and sandstone bedrock at our feet.

Arches. In 2007, on a trip to visit Katherine's mother in California, we made a quick stop in Arches. We had first visited Arches nearly 40 years earlier, about the same time I discovered Edward Abbey's classic Desert Solitaire. Seeing it on this quick visit was like coming home.

Lost in the Rocks of Time. Living in Bicknell while working on the Dixie National Forest, I spent much of my free time exploring Boulder Mountain and Thousand Lake Mountain, much of which was part of the land I was administering. I had found a hidden and rarely visited chunk of BLM land right next to my home. It took a climb hand over foot to make it through the Wingate cliffs, but once above them, I was on a nearly flat plateau that skirted the base of Thousand Lake Mountain. My goal was to eventually climb the bump on the side of the mountain that locals referred to as the Anthill. I never made it since every time I went a little further, it seems the anthill grew a little further away and taller in size. One trip, I discovered a small rock overhang which sheltered two pristine petroglyph panels. The next trip, Katherine did drawings of the panels and we have used one of the images in several occasions, in her artwork and my writing. I never spent a day living in this slickrock paradise without marveling over the geology and the aspect of geologic time.

October Storm. On another trip to Moab, we got caught in a deluge, where rivers of red mud literally ran alongside the highway. This was the type of storm that would catch you in a deadly flash flood if you happened to be in a slot canyon. The fury of this quick flying storm matched the power of the canyon country itself. The two merged into a force that humbled me and inspired me to write.

Clouds of Heaven. After retirement, I stayed active in the wildland fire system. I was red carded (qualified) as a Public Information Officer and usually traveled to several major fires a year. This often required flying out of either Grand Junction or Montrose. Whether the flight was to Denver or Salt Lake City and points further, it was in the summer, which meant monsoon season. Flights were often quite bumpy as we would go over, around, or through thunderstorms over the mountains. One trip to Salt Lake, as we approached the Wasatch Front, we hit the daily storms. I had never seen a display of clouds so impressive. We zigged and zagged as we went between towering cells. It was magical and surreal as we kissed the edges of clouds and maneuvered between them before finally having to plow straight through.

Bodega Head. I have never spent much time on the coast and even less on the ocean itself. The few times I visited coasts, I gravitated to the rocky and rugged coastlines of Washington, Oregon and California. To me, these have the same intrigue and pull canyons and mountains do. The relentless roll of the surf, the pounding on rocks and cliffs, are the force of untamed nature. One trip to California, I found refuge along the Sonoma coast. As I stood on the cliff at Bodega Head watching the Pacific roll and thunder beneath me, I noticed the bouquet of wildflowers at my feet. This intrigued me. As I watched seals bob in the surf and cormorants laze on a rock cliff, I wondered what the story was behind this simply act of emotion.

Stinson Beach. On a visit to the Bay area in 2004, I found myself at Stinson Beach near Muir Woods. My thoughts were more on the sandy beach and the sea gulls. This took me back to 1968 when my college roommate and I drove down to the Bay area to visit my fiancé over Christmas break. After running a red light on San Francisco's Market Street with four people in my pickup truck cab

on New Year's Eve, we drove on up to Stinson Beach. To
a flatlander from Illinois who had only seen the ocean
once or twice in my life, this was a magical trip. Throwing
rocks at seagulls was my idea of impressing a girl. I was
very wrong about that. This second visit was my chance to
reflect on that and apologize to the birds.

Muir Woods. During the 2007 trip, I needed the energy
that only redwoods could provide. Another force of nature,
besides mountains, canyons and seacoasts, the power of
these massive and ancient living things create an awe that
some people only get from religious experiences. Sitting
in a grove of these trees renewed my spirit. Although not
as old and massive as the groves further north, these still
inspired me. I had to find a secluded place away from the
masses of tourists walking the main paved trail below me.
I could not understand their indifference to this holy place.
They were just walking the trail, not even looking up or
stopping to enjoy what silence they might find. Even with
people nearby, I still found the solitude and peace I sought.

Laughingwater. I named a portion of a spring fed creek
on my own property in Western Colorado, Laughingwater.
This was the name of a stream that fed the Ohanapecosh
River in Mt. Rainier National Park. I worked the trail
crew at Ohana for two summers while in and fresh out
of college. My own creek provides a peaceful setting to
retreat to whenever I need a break. It is my own hidden
water paradise that sits in its small wilderness. No one
goes there unless they are our guests at our Retreat and
I am usually with them. I can count on finding solitude,
along with an occasional cougar, bobcat, deer or rabbit.
In the winter, the countless seeps and springs feeding
the stream freeze and sculpt the hillsides with artistic ice

flows. A rare type of orchid grows on the watery hillsides, adding more of nature's grace to the setting.

A Water Journey. Several years ago, I was an Art Partner for a young man who wanted help with writing. I designed a program having him come to our Retreat and write about nature. One day, I explained the cycle of water and asked him to write about it. Later, I thought "I should write this myself." Thus my imaginary journey of a water droplet from ocean to land to plant to animal back to ocean, illustrating the complexity of natural cycles.

Assembly of Angels. Every spring we marvel at the return of the sandhill cranes on their migration from either the San Luis Valley of Colorado or further south in New Mexico. They fly directly over our house and either keep going north or veer west and overnight at Fruitgrowers Reservoir about 15 miles from us. We drive down to the reservoir at least once a spring to watch them land.

Jornada of the Ravens. We occasionally see flocks of ravens, especially in the winter, but this was extraordinary. We have ravens nest in the springtime on our property. They are loud so you always know where they are. It is comical to see the young ravens all perched on the top of a juniper, three or four black dots bobbing back and forth nestled in a clump of green. There is a pecking order of birds. Ravens chase hawks and eagles, magpies chase ravens, jays chase magpies. You can tell when an owl or bobcat is around by the ravens and magpies screaming and dive bombing. Life is tough all around.

The Last Grizzly. A local whom I had never met called me one winter day with a question. The contractor who built our house told him I was a wildlife biologist and I might know. So the rugged outdoorsman came by with the photos and a cast of the paw print. It was huge. He was in the process of trying to get a university professor, expert on grizzlies, to comment on the print. He wanted to know if I thought it was a grizzly. I had no idea, but if it was a black bear, it was monstrous. I knew all the experts said there was no way there were any more grizzlies in Colorado, but as I always say, "the animals don't read textbooks," so you never know for sure about wildlife. Whether or not it was a griz (probably not), the thought intrigued me. I wish so much to be able to get inside the mind of one of the last of its kind.

When the Hummingbirds Leave. The hummingbird is one of my favorite birds. They arrive like clockwork, but leave sporadically. We always look forward to their arrival on April 21, give or take a day. By the time the first breezes of late August signal autumn, I feel sad they are slowly leaving. Often, one or two hang on for a couple weeks, worrying me that they may not heed their instinct. They always do. Then there are none and I wait a week to take down the feeders. The turning of the aspen, the first killing frost, then hard freeze take my attention away from the hummingbirds, and by the first snow, I have moved on. But come April, I am looking again at the calendar, awaiting the whirr of wings.

Buttercup. In my entire Forest Service career, I never saw a mountain lion, even though I was out in the woods quite a lot. Since we now live in deer winter range and have a dozen or more deer hanging around the house all winter, I know there are cats watching me whenever I hike around the property. In the almost 25 years we have owned the property, I have seen three mountain lions, twice sitting within ten feet of the door of the house or lodge. Few people ever see them, so it is a privilege to see one; it is a spiritual experience to find a dead one like I did and be able to touch her and look in detail at her body. Goldberry and I first knew of her presence when she was still alive, but obviously sick. The dog was going crazy barking and I found a very fresh track, with sides of the track in the snow still crumbling into the footprint. Although we didn't see her, we beat a hasty exit, but for the next month, every time I let Goldberry out at night for her chores, I felt a strange sensation. Something was out there. We found the body a month after that first encounter. We called the game warden and he wanded her, finding no evidence of a bullet. He later came to take her away and reported that the necropsy indicated severe dehydration and diarrhea. She was a young female that never had kittens. That experience affected me in a way that combined respect, awe, fear, and the indifference of nature.

The First Sunflower. The wild sunflower is a regular around here, found along roadsides and disturbed soil. It is a cornucopia for wildlife, with the insects and birds loving the pollen, then birds and squirrels feasting on the abundant seeds. Like its domestic cousin, the flowerhead follows the sun, turning from east to west during the day, until the maturing flower finally stops and gets serious about maturing the seeds.

Butterfly Migration. I first saw a butterfly migration in California's Sierra Nevada. Thousands came flying by at eye level, undulating with the uneven ground as they flew from west to east. Then, at our place in western Colorado, I saw butterflies coming uphill, crossing the ridgetop, then going downhill to the next ridge. I use the word 'flying' cautiously, however. Butterflies are said to fly, but they flitter, they bounce, they somehow move through the air. They make it work, but it never ceases to amaze me how they do it.

Homestake. The underground Homestake mine no longer exists; it is now flooded forever with millions of gallons of water. Several years ago, the mine officials must have finally realized the cost of digging deeper and deeper was not worth the tremendous cost. So I feel privileged to have been able to tour the depths of the mine in 1992. The feeling of going so deep was surreal. The surface of the Black Hills has its own magic. This is where east meets west, south meets north. A bubble on the Great Plains. Ample rainfall and good soil, it grows trees and grass, elk and deer, and once upon a time, herds of bison. Gold is what Custer discovered and what brought the throngs of white settlers and gold seekers who desecrated what was sacred to Lakota and generations of natives before they came West. My vow to never again buy any gold jewelry came from the amazement of what people will do to take this gold metal from the ground.

Weathered Dreams. I wrote this to accompany an etching my wife did back in the mid 70's. The cabin was somewhere on the edges of North Park in northern Colorado. We gave the etching along with my essay to my mother for Christmas one year. It hung on the living room wall of my folk's house until I took it down when I cleaned the house after their deaths. Back in the days we first saw the cabin, we could still find settlers' and prospectors' cabins in the forests that I managed. Now, over 40 years later, I doubt if much is left standing, but the cabins were tough, just like the people who built them.

Leaning Cabin. Like the weathered cabin in the previous essay, this was from the same general area. Again, it served as the model of one of Katherine's etchings and my essay. The history they could tell.....

Lance Creek, Wyoming. These thoughts originated in October 1993 as I drove a lonely stretch of Wyoming road, listening to an "oldies" radio station out of western Nebraska. The time of year, the empty landscape, the nostalgia created by 1960's music all combined to create a reflective mood tying together meanings and values of this place. Before I could put my thoughts on paper the next day, I received word of my mother's death. I didn't write my reflections from that October day. After that, I traveled this stretch of road several times. Each time, I listened to that same radio station. I never felt the same emotions as I did that very first time. Finally, I took a tape recorder and recorded my original thoughts as I tried to recollect them. It was June 1994 and I was returning from a workshop in Estes Park, Colorado. I had suffered food poisoning the night before and cut short my attendance, driving the 7 hours home in a very shaky state of health. My thoughts on this lonely piece of country are dedicated to Ruby Marie Hance Colwell.

Dragonfly. There is an old pond on the creek below my house. The water is entirely spring fed, so it is pure and cold. Cattails fill the stream and watercress fills the pond. On a hot summer day, the pond is filled with frogs, water striders, damselflies and dragonflies. It is prehistoric and cool. I am in the middle of space and time when I stand there by myself.

The Weather Station. For years I have been recording the weather every day. High and low temperatures as well as rain or snow. I always wanted one of those old wooden, slatted weather stations to put the thermometer inside to keep it out of the sun. I finally got one from the National Weather Service in Grand Junction. I scraped it, painted it, and put it up. It has stood faithfully for over ten years. I thought about where it had been for decades before it came to me. This was my fantasy.

Glenwood Canyon. This was a half hour during one spring day on the start of a trip to Illinois to visit my dad. You cannot make this up.

The Smoke of Summer. For the last ten years of my Forest Service career, and for 12 years after retirement, I served as a Public Information Officer on fires and other incidents across the West. Over the July 4th holiday in 2008, I traveled to Willows, California for an assignment. The trip had been crazy, missing a plane in Phoenix and staying overnight near the airport, then missing my luggage on the trip to Sacramento. Exhausted on the final leg of the trip, I was talking to myself on the drive up to Willows. The air was full of smoke, the sunflower fields lined the highway. On all these assignments, I never knew what I was getting into. These were my thoughts on this trip.

Flight of the Cattail Down. Sitting above the creek near the dragonfly pond below my house on a November afternoon, I was mesmerized by the cattails shedding their seeds. This is now a yearly ritual of autumn meditation.

Aspen Gold. I was spoiled by my first Forest Service assignment. We lived along the Conejos River west of the San Luis Valley in southern Colorado. This was aspen country. Aspen in pure stands or mixed with spruce, it was a beauty any time of year, but especially in the autumn. I will never forget those September days of 1970, a bright blue sky highlighting the gold and white aspen. Every autumn, I return to those dreams of heaven and try to find something nearby that approaches the fantasy.

Aspen in the Rocks of Heaven. My wife asked me to write some poems that she could stitch to one of her embroidered art works. So one autumn day, we drove to the top of Grand Mesa at a secluded spot along the western rim near Land's End. While she drew, the dog and I wandered among the rocks, thinking and writing. Some of these stanzas are now written in thread as the aspen bark texture.

Mt. Rainier Fantasy. In the summers of 1968 and 1969, I worked for the National Park Service on the trail crew out of the Ohanapecosh District. I lived in the seasonal employee compound at the Ohana Ranger Station, miles from anywhere. The summer was magical. The mountain was magical and the people were magical. That is where I met Katherine. I will forever remember those two summers as highlights of my life.

Silence. One of the benefits of living on our 40 acre retreat is the relative isolation. We have no neighbor within ¼ mile and very few within a half mile. I can spend all day by myself listening to the wind, the creek, the birds. I don't understand why more people don't turn off their cell phones, I-pods, and other noisemakers and just listen to the quiet. It allows creativity and peace for the soul.

I Know There is a God. I have always loved a variety of music and listen to it when I write. On occasion, I have played music while driving or camping in some remote location. Certain artists and music, when combined with these magical settings, enhance the experience.

A Wilderness of the Soul. I like the idea of official Wilderness, but don't understand why people cannot find their own secluded spot to get that wilderness feeling. Like many other things, we carry it with us wherever we go. Just let your imagination carry you miles further.

Sun Stands Still. The winter solstice has been important to people for millennia. I find it fascinating that primitive peoples were able to determine this important date by casting shadows or rocks or shrines. People lived by circles and cycles. How many religious holidays are centered around this important and symbolic date of rebirth?

Lazuli. The lazuli buntings arrive every spring just a few days after the first hummingbird. We have had as many as nine males at the feeder at one time. They are shy and quiet and dainty eaters. Their colors are rich and luminous, mirroring the earth, sky, and clouds.

The Pollinators. I never paid much attention to bees and bugs, but in the summer, when all our flowers are in bloom, I am amazed at the variety of insects that pollinate our flowers. Some are delicate like the lacewings, some colorful like the butterflies, some powerful like the praying mantis. And then there are the bees—countless varieties from the massive bumblebee to a tiny green bee.

ABOUT THE AUTHOR

 When the West called, Joseph Colwell left the flat prairies of central Illinois for the University of Idaho. During his college years, he spent summers working in Idaho state parks, Mt. Rainier National Park, and Grand Canyon National Park. With his degree in wildlife management, he spent the next 27 years with the US Forest Service.

He worked on five different national forests across the West, managing and exploring the land. He helped bring moose into Colorado, peregrine falcons into the northern Sierra, and created a program of guided hikes under the full moon in South Dakota. Retiring from his Forest Service career, he continued work as a Fire Information Officer on wildland fires, assisting the general public and homeowners with understanding wildfires.

Joseph and his artist wife Katherine now live on their 40-acre nature preserve overlooking the North Fork Valley of western Colorado. They created Colwell Cedars Retreat, offering a peaceful, secluded haven for guests as well as local wildlife. While not working on his property, Joseph is guiding hikes on his four miles of trails, tending the organic garden with Katherine, reading, and enjoying the retreat's mesa with its spectacular views of the San Juan Mountains and West Elk Wilderness. He can be reached at ColwellCedars.com

CPSIA information can be obtained
at www.ICGtesting.com
Printed in the USA
FSHW02n2028120618
49351FS